# God Alone

## Stories of the Power of Faith

Angela Burrin and Patricia Mitchell
General Editors

Partners in
Evangelism

A Ministry of *The Word Among Us*

The Word Among Us Press
9639 Doctor Perry Road
Ijamsville, Maryland 21754
ISBN: 0-932085-44-X

www.wau.org

©2000 by The Word Among Us Press
Second printing 2002

Design by David Crosson

Made and printed in the United States of America

# God Alone

## Stories of the Power of Faith

# Dear Friends in Christ:

*I say to the LORD, you are my Lord, you are my only good.*
(Psalm 16:2)

The psalmist realized an important truth that many in the world fail to see. Only in God can we find true peace and joy. The world and all its pleasures can make us happy for a while, but in the deepest core of our being, we can only be fulfilled by God. God is our only good, yet we erect a host of idols that keep us distracted and away from the ultimate source of our happiness. We can so easily keep God on the sidelines, thinking of him perhaps on Sundays at Mass or at important events like baptisms and weddings. Yet when we limit God in this way, we limit the love and power he offers to us every moment of every day. The purpose of this book is to show what happens when we invite God into our hearts and give him permission to truly be the Lord of our lives.

*God Alone: Stories of the Power of Faith* is a testament to a God who is real, a God who works in power in the world today, a God who is with us at all times. Written by ordinary people who have faced extraordinary challenges, these stories help us to see God in a new way. They provide a portrait of the Lord that may surprise us because we may have underestimated what he can do, for us and through us, when we reach out to him. The men and women who have written these stories are each in their own way modern-day prophets, proclaiming to a skeptical world that God is alive, and that he wants to breathe his life into us, both now and forever.

This book is a joint project of *The Word Among Us Press* and *Partners in Evangelism*, a ministry that raises funds to donate solid spiritual materials to prisoners. Through this ministry, 20,000 prisoners in the United States and Canada currently receive these materials each month. Our goal was to publish a book that could be distributed free of charge to prisoners and that could also inspire men and women in all walks of life to a greater love and appreciation of our Father. As always, we want everyone to know that God's love is unconditional and that it has the power to change lives. One of the best ways we know of accomplishing this goal is through the stories of those who have been transformed—and healed—by the saving power of Jesus Christ. God has no better witnesses than those whose hearts he has touched.

These stories differ in many ways. Some are about conversion, some are about healing, others are about acceptance or discovery. However, the common thread among them is that God never abandons us, even in our darkest hour. The men and women you will meet in these pages don't have the answer to why there is suffering in the world. However, they do show us how we can respond when we face similar circumstances, because in every case, they turned to God and asked him for his help and deliverance. In a myriad of ways, he heard their cries and manifested himself to them, comforting them and bringing them peace.

Thus, the title of this book: *God Alone*. He alone brings us joy; he alone forgives our sins and heals our souls, no matter how unworthy we feel. He alone is the "living water" that will quench our thirst forever (John 4:10-15). For some of the men and women in this book, especially those who are in prison, it took losing everything—their freedom, their jobs, their families, their friends—to realize that God was still waiting to embrace them with loving arms. Like St. Paul, that gift made all their loss turn to gain (Philippians 3:8).

We wish to thank all the contributors to this book who have given us permission to publish their stories. Some of the writers requested that we not print their complete names, and we have honored their requests. In every case, however, the authors were excited about the opportunity to share about God's love and faithfulness.

Let these stories of faith encourage you. If you desire a closer relationship with God—the kind of relationship the people in this book have found—then ask Jesus into your life. He knocks at the door of our hearts, but he will never force himself in. When we open the door, we find our best friend, our beloved, one who is completely trustworthy and faithful, one who will never leave us. If you already enjoy a close intimacy with God, then pass this book along to a friend or neighbor. Together, let us proclaim the goodness of our Lord, whose steadfast love endures forever! (Psalm 136:1).

Angela Burrin
Director
*Partners in Evangelism*

Patricia Mitchell
Editor
*The Word Among Us Press*

# 1

# On God's Death Row

## by Michael B. Ross

*Take heed, watch; for you do not know when
the time will come.* (Mark 13:33)

I'm sure that you have been told at one time or another that all of us, in a sense, live on death row. It is a favorite topic of many preachers. Human beings are mortal, and death is inevitable. As such, death is life's most powerful enemy, no matter who we are—no matter how wealthy, how powerful, how blessed—we all will eventually succumb to death. Instinctively, all of us resist death with every fiber of our beings. This is completely natural and to be expected.

Are you prepared for death? Have you thought about that day when there are no more tomorrows? Many of us have not. That is because many of us fear death; it is a very difficult topic for us to deal with, so we ignore its very possibility. Many of us try to deny its power, its inevitability, its very existence. When it does come, usually unexpectedly, we are generally unprepared.

**Facing My Mortality.** I live on death row. Not exactly the same death row that the preachers will tell you that you live on. Mine is far more concrete, far more immediate. I am to be executed by the State of Connecticut. I will know, to within a few minutes, the exact day and time that I will die.

I will know the exact day and time that I will meet Christ. And while I expect that this may sound strange, this has been a great blessing to me.

I have been forced to face my own mortality. I have been blessed with time to try to set things right and make my peace with God. I have been given time to ask and seek forgiveness from those whom I have hurt. I have been given time for my own hurts to be healed and to forgive those who have hurt me. My time is coming, and I have been given time to prepare for my meeting with Christ. It is a blessing that few are fortunate to experience.

Don't misunderstand me: I don't look forward to my execution. I don't welcome the prospect of death. I have my own concerns and fears about it, as I suspect we all do. Everyone fears the unknown, and death is the greatest of unknowns. Every day, I pray that some miracle will come to pass which will deliver me from this man-made death row and spare me from the hands of a human executioner. I would like a second chance at life; anyone in my situation would. However, should I not get that chance, I am at least fortunate enough to have had time to prepare for my death.

**How Will We Live?** I recently read about a Christian who was dying of pancreatic cancer. He wrote some wonderful words that I take great comfort in—words that I have made into a personal prayer of mine. I try to live by these words and I would like to share them with you:

> *My future is uncertain. The joy is knowing that it is completely in God's hands. All I have to do is thank him. If I have not much longer to live, then that is God's will and*

*it should mean something. My task is to find out what it means. I have no complaints, only thanks! If it is God's pleasure to give me a chance to start over again, that's wonderful. If it is not his pleasure and he has other tasks for me, I accept that. Faith doesn't depend upon me having my way; faith depends on God having his way. This must be my highest joy and delight. Otherwise, how can I pray, "Thy will be done"?*

Few of us will have the blessing of knowing the hour of our death. But each of us must still face his own mortality. Each of us must prepare for his own death. The question is: How do we do that?

This may sound paradoxical, but preparation for death is not a matter of how we die, but a matter of how we live. It is the great promise of Christ that as we live, so shall we die. To live for Christ means that we must be prepared to die every single day of our lives. For if we are prepared to die daily for Christ, we will receive eternal life and our promised salvation.

To truly prepare for death, we must live each day as if it were our last. We must live that day for Christ. This is more difficult than it sounds; it is very easy to be distracted and count on tomorrow always being there. We must not allow ourselves to be distracted; we must not count on tomorrow. Instead, we are to remember our own mortality and our purpose for being. As the Indian mystic Sundar Singh said: "Only during the few years of this life are we given the privilege of serving each other and Christ. We will have heaven forever, but have only a short time for service here, and therefore must not waste the opportunity." These words tell us not to waste the few glorious opportunities that we have to live for Christ.

**Cherish Each Day.** This is easier for me to do than it is for most people. I have the specter of death always hanging over my head. I will meet Christ soon. Every morning when I wake up, I try to recall that I have few opportunities left to serve Christ here in this world. I try hard not to count on tomorrow, because I may have few tomorrows left.

I didn't always think this way. Twenty years ago I was a young man heading off to an Ivy League college. Like most people that age, I didn't often ponder my mortality. In many ways I felt immortal; I assumed that tomorrow would always be there. As I sit alone here in this cell, I look back on those youthful days with anguish. Today, I can remember all the lost opportunities of yesterday. I see the things that I could have done and should have done, things I always intended to do "tomorrow." It is terrible to feel that you have wasted your life. It is a terrible feeling I pray you will never experience.

Don't count on tomorrow. Cherish and live each day as if it were your last. Live the life that God has given to you to its fullest potential. And live each day that God has given you for his glory. Don't forget Jesus' teaching about the two greatest commandments: "Love the Lord your God with all your heart, and with all your soul, and with all your mind. . . . Love your neighbor as yourself" (Matthew 22:37,39). Not just sometimes, not just when you have the time and it is convenient. Every day!

Your next encounter with your neighbor may be your last. Seek forgiveness and forgive those who have hurt you. Not tomorrow—today! Repent to God for your past transgressions and live each day to further his glory. Now, right this minute; tomorrow may never come. If you live each day as if it were your last, you need not worry about death. You will be prepared for that day when it comes, even if it comes unexpectedly.

**Join Me in Prayer.** I live on death row, and I would like to invite you to join me. Not here on Connecticut's death row—there are too many of us here already—but on God's death row. For when you live on God's death row, you live for God, for his glory, every day. You may not be fortunate enough to know when your death is at hand, but you will be prepared.

Are you prepared to meet Jesus? Are you ready to stand before God to give an account of your life? Are you ready, especially if death should strike suddenly? Are you living on God's death row? If you accept my invitation to live on God's death row, then please join me in a prayer from the Way of the Cross, a prayer that has much meaning for me, and that I hope will have as much meaning for you:

*My Lord Jesus, you laid your life down for me. I will lay down my life for you. I offer you my death with all the pain that may surround it, accepting at this moment, whatever kind of death you have in store for me. I give you my life and my death, my body and soul, my whole being now and forever.* ■

# 2

# Only a Prayer Away

## by Mary S.

Every year, millions of Americans suffer from a disease known as bipolar disorder, or manic-depressive disorder. I am one of the many who suffer with this debilitating disease. A large percentage of the men and women with this form of mental illness are able to lead productive lives with the help of proper treatment. But there are also people who look just fine outwardly but struggle inside day to day to make sense of something that no sense can be made of. These individuals can't hold down jobs and can only hope to lead some semblance of a normal existence. The constant battles with the ups and downs of this affliction are staggering and exhausting. Unfortunately, I fall into the small percentage of persons for which medications and other forms of treatment do not seem to help. My life is a constant, uphill battle.

As long as I can remember I have suffered from depressive episodes. For the longest time I could not understand why this illness still haunted me. I have a happy home, a loving husband and two children, and yet I was in a constant state of inner turmoil and agony. Anything I could ever want or need was at my disposal. Why wasn't I happy? With the exception of my immediate family, no one was aware of the emotional pain I was enduring. All my friends envied me because I seemed to have everything life could offer. But I felt so alone, so helpless. Through years of extensive therapy, I now know that my battle with bipolar disorder is a chemical imbalance in my brain and something that I will have to deal with the rest of my life.

**"Have Mercy, Lord!"** I had become very good at putting on my "happy face" until one day in December of 1990, when things came to a head. I was no longer able to handle the bouts of despair. I had always considered myself a good Catholic and a good Christian, but now my faith was starting to waver. I was losing sight of God and his wondrous deeds. Why had he inflicted such a terrible disease on me? What had I done to deserve his wrath? Was I being punished for my sins? Was I that bad of a person? Why me, God? These were the thoughts that flooded my mind morning and night. I felt I was a burden to my husband and my children. They deserved so much better than me. I even felt abandoned by the Lord and I could no longer find solace in his word.

In the midst of my despair, I took an overdose of prescription medications, hoping to relieve my constant inner turmoil. I had lost all hope. I had lost my faith. Nothing anyone said to me made any sense or difference at the time. It seemed to me that no matter how hard I tried to please people, I always failed. Nothing I did was good enough. I was so busy trying to please everyone else that I forgot about myself. I was ready to die, and the sooner the better.

One morning I awoke, sent my family off on various errands and, after swallowing numerous pills, proceeded to write my suicide letter. I lay on my bed quietly, waiting for the effects of the medication to start. The entire time I could hear myself praying Psalm 6:3—"Have pity on me,

O Lord, for I am languishing; heal me, O Lord, for my body is in terror." I repeated these words over and over in my mind while tears trickled down my face. These were my last thoughts before I slipped into oblivion.

I knew that taking my own life was an unforgivable sin, but at the time I did not care. I just wanted peace and consolation. I wanted someone to wrap his arms around me, to hold me tightly, and never let go. I wanted and needed love, but I felt that I had no one.

**A Miraculous Protection.** The doctors told my husband to gather the family together because they doubted that I would make it through the night. And if I did somehow pull through, I would probably have major brain and/or lung dysfunction. Miraculously, I did not die or suffer any side effects. I attribute this to the fact that God heard my prayers after all. When I had given up, he had not. I realized when I had awakened from my deep sleep that the Lord had never left my side. I had doubted God, but—thankfully—he is a forgiving and understanding God. He allowed me to live as a testimony of his love and devotion to his children here on earth. I knew that God had forgiven me for my attempted suicide because I was not in a right state of mind at the time.

When I woke up three days later, I looked out the window of my room in the intensive care unit and could not help but admire the beautiful blue sky. Something strange and different was stirring in me. Everything seemed to be new. The trees were such a deep shade of brown, the clouds like white tufts of cotton floating through the sky. I felt as though I was looking into the Garden of Eden. God had truly created a beautiful world for us.

**Finding Strength in God's Word.** Since then, I have had occasional setbacks and days and nights filled with tears over my disorder. But I no longer ask God "Why?" As Psalm 40:2 says, "I have waited, waited for the Lord, and he stooped toward me and heard my cry." When I have that familiar feeling of despair and hopelessness, I read Scripture and find great comfort and strength.

I have come to accept my illness and have stopped blaming everyone and everything for it. Because of this affliction, I feel I am becoming a better Christian. I no longer read the Bible only with my eyes, but with my heart as well, as God intended us to do. God never leaves our side. We are the ones who question him. We are an impatient people.

Sirach 2:2-4 says: "Be sincere of heart and steadfast, undisturbed in time of adversity. Cling to him, forsake him not; thus will your future be great. Accept whatever befalls you, in crushing misfortune be patient." If only we could all see and come to the understanding that God is never far from our grasp. He lives eternally in his word and is always there for us, whether we realize it or not. It may take some drastic situation to convince us that God will never abandon us—that he is only a prayer away.

Because of my human weakness, I must remind myself that God always hears my plea: "Though I am afflicted and poor, yet the Lord thinks of me. You are my help and my deliverer; O my God, hold not back!" (Psalm 40:18). The Lord is my deliverer. He alone brought me back from the gates of death. He has put me on the right path. I have put my illness into his hands and allowed him to carry me from day to day. Truly God is only a prayer away. ■

3

# Rescue Me, Lord!

**by Violetta Slizh**

I have always felt that life itself is so miraculous that supernatural events weren't really necessary for faith. But all the same, miracles happen. It is a miracle that I can breathe, move, work, and be an instrument in the hands of my Creator. It is a miracle that God came into my life and healed me of a debilitating disease. It is a miracle, too, that we are never alone. Jesus gives us the strength to live. He is always with us.

**Discovering My Emptiness.** I have always loved horses; I grew up riding and taking care of them. However, one day in 1978, when I was twenty years old, I was riding and my horse threw me. The fall injured my head and upper spinal column. Up until then, I had everything I thought I had ever longed for—interesting work, success, money, and adventure. I was surrounded by numerous friends and admirers. Everything I did turned out well. But the accident gave me a chance to think about the purpose of my life and about God. Sometimes feelings of emptiness seized me, and my attempts to fill this emptiness were unsuccessful.

A couple of years later, I moved to Tbilisi in Georgia. There was a Catholic church there—one of the few in the Soviet Union—and I remember going to visit it one day. At the church, I met a woman with kind eyes who tried to explain to me the truths of the faith. Looking back, I realize she was probably an underground nun who would have been sent to a slave camp if word got out about who she was. Despite this woman's words, I couldn't make sense of the odd rituals. The sign of the cross and the practice of kneeling down before the tabernacle and the altar seemed especially to be ridiculous anachronisms. In reality, pride was preventing me from seeing that the church is God's house. I told myself that church is for weak people, and that I didn't need it. I could find God inside myself, on my own.

A year later, I left Tbilisi and moved to Kharkov, in the far eastern part of Ukraine. For some reason, on my first day there, I combed the center of town in search of a Catholic church. When I found one, I felt happy, but as I approached it, I saw that it was being used instead for a regional government office. There was no altar. There was no woman with kind eyes waiting to talk to me about faith. It would be twelve more years before this building would be returned to the church. I thought I had found God inside myself, but alone, outside of the church, it is not possible to keep him.

In the meantime, my health was failing. Three years after my accident, I started experiencing headaches and weakness. Every six months, I would end up in the hospital for tests and treatments, but the suffering continued.

**Rescue Me!** My enlightenment occurred unexpectedly. During a trip to Krakow, Poland, I visited the Marian church there to see a famous altar made by Witus Stwosz—

something I had heard about for a long time and longed to see. Little did I realize what God had in store for me. In one very intense moment, I understood everything about myself and about God. I could not leave the church. I remained there until the evening praying, for the first time speaking with Christ as my Lord. It was painful to recognize the truth about myself. I cried out, "O Lord, I am weak and sinful, but rescue me! Save me from myself! I cannot live without you!" The emptiness had reached its limit, and I cried out to the Lord to save me.

Finally, on April 17, 1991, the church in Kharkov re-opened, and three weeks later I crossed its threshold. Holy Communion seemed strange to me, and my hands and legs felt like wood and refused to bend before the Lord. But as I prayed before the Blessed Sacrament, my legs finally did bend by themselves and I kneeled down before the hidden Jesus. The feeling of love that I experienced continued even after I left the church, and stayed with me in the office, at home, on the train or bus—everywhere I went. I understood that "He who eats my flesh and drinks my blood abides in me, and I in him" (John 6:56). On May 29, I received my first Holy Communion. Though I recognized how unworthy I was, I also realized that I could not live without Jesus.

In early 1995, when I was thirty-eight years old, I was diagnosed with multiple sclerosis. The gloomy prognosis—blindness, deafness, losing the mobility of my arms and legs, and an early death—was no longer a remote possibility, but very close at hand. Earlier, I had thought that I could endure any trial. What a delusion! I felt unable to endure it any longer. I was a burden to my friends and family members, and I wanted my life to end as soon as possible.

**Fighting Despair.** My one consolation was in the Passion of Christ. His crucifixion was constantly before my eyes, and I united my sufferings with him. At the time, I didn't understand that my pride was keeping me from asking for healing. However, I didn't think that healing was possible. The doctors had told me that my illness was incurable, and I was too pragmatic and rational to believe in miracles. They only happened during Jesus' earthly life. However, a priest, Father Miroslaw, would visit me once a week and give me Jesus hidden in the bread. The Eucharist gave me strength not to despair completely, and to hold out a little longer.

During one of those long evenings of pain and sadness, I came across this Scripture: "Come, let us return to Yahweh. He has rent us and he will heal us; he has struck us and he will bind up our wounds; after two days he will revive us, on the third day he will raise us up and we shall live in his presence" (Hosea 6:1-2). I felt a glimmer of hope.

It was late autumn. The cold weather had settled in and the sky was a transparent blue. In the woods near my house, however, among the brown dry leaves there were small violet flowers and bright emerald grasses. I thought, "Maybe it's because I won't see another spring that the Lord is giving me a glimpse of it now." But for some reason, I wasn't afraid. I had found peace.

**Victory in the Blood of Jesus.** Then, on the last Thursday in November, Father Miroslaw visited me with three friends from church, along with three people from the Protestant church whom I had never met before. Father Miroslaw asked me, "Do you want to be healed?"

"Yes," I answered. "But it's impossible. My illness is incurable."

"But our God is the Lord of all. It is in his power to give you health! Do you believe that Jesus loves you and doesn't want you to suffer?"

"Yes, I believe."

And the work began. While it is difficult to describe what was going through my mind for the next two hours, I remember praying, "Jesus, I believe that you are living, risen and now acting in the same way as you did two thousand years ago. Send your Spirit, the Spirit of healing!" I knew that the Lord had promised that if two or three come together in his name, he would be among them. "Be with us, Jesus!"

Then, in an instant, the small room where I was lying became huge. I had a vision of many people, not just the seven people who were physically there, but thousands who prayed to the Lord. And Jesus came! He looked like Sister Faustina's portrait of Divine Mercy. Blood was running from his pierced hands, and as he touched my head, I was overcome with joy. His blood soaked in me, washed my brain, and poured down my body. It was dissolving everything that was harmful or unnecessary.

The skin on my hands and legs became sensitive again, and my spine resumed its natural form. My left leg, which was one centimeter shorter than the other, became as long as the right one. The miracle happened! Our voices merged in song: "He has given us a victory! The evil one is defeated! Death does not reign any more! Jesus is our Lord! Hallelujah!" One week later, I was examined by my doctors, who could find nothing wrong with me. I was completely healthy.

**Set Free to Serve.** I strongly believe that Jesus didn't just heal me for my own sake. He opened doors for me to give my life to him in service. On the very weekend that I was healed, my good friend Irina was in Warsaw making arrangements for herself and me to begin translating and publishing *The Word Among Us* for the people of Ukraine. Now, four years later, we have more than two thousand readers, both in Ukraine and other former Soviet Bloc countries.

Since that day, I have reflected on Jesus' healing of the paralytic (Mark 2:1-12). I thought that if I should be brought to Jesus, I would not find just four friends, but many more. I am grateful to everyone who has helped me believe in the risen Christ: to all my friends, known and unknown, who prayed and "stripped the roof" (2:4)—not only in Ukraine, but also in Russia, Poland, Spain, Sweden, and everywhere.

O Lord, I no longer belong to myself. My life is your life, for my life is already finished, and the new one you have given me belongs completely to you. ■

# 4

# God Gave Me a New Family

**by C.K.**

Shortly after I was born, my mother decided to give me up for adoption. Fortunately, her parents (my grandparents) were willing to take me in and raise me. They did the best they could with me, even sending me to a Catholic grade school. Then, when I was about ten years old, my grandfather died and my mom moved in with my grandmother—along with my stepfather and stepbrothers and stepsisters. As a result, I was kind of kicked out and went to live with my widowed aunt on the next street.

I was alone often because my aunt had to work to support us. Still, she was very good to me. Both she and my grandmother wanted me to go to a Catholic high school, but the seeds of rebellion had already been planted in me, and I let them grow.

**Feeling Rejected.** For the longest time, I was searching for a place to fit in, because I never felt like I fit in anywhere at all. So, when I was about fourteen years old, I started to drink beer to fit in with the local kids. The world was changing quickly in the 1960s, and my buddies started to do a lot of bad things. Their need for drug money had turned them to burglary, and so I started hanging around less and less with them. I felt even more that I was a reject and that I didn't fit in anywhere.

I tried living with my father in Alabama a few times, but he had a cold attitude toward me. I got the impression from both my dad and mom that I was a constant reminder to them of their failed marriage—as if it were my fault. I was searching so hard for someplace to fit in, something solid to belong to, and I couldn't find it. Eventually, I quit school.

**A Downward Spiral.** At seventeen years old, I joined the Marines, but that only made things worse. I went from being scared and insecure to being arrogant and hardened. When I got discharged, I moved to Pennsylvania—still searching for a place to fit in—and ended up marrying the sister of a buddy of mine from the Marines. We were blessed by God with a beautiful son, but our marriage only lasted about one and a half years. We broke up mainly because of my drinking, self-centeredness, and temper. Even though I had a family, I was still searching for something to fill the emptiness inside of me, and I had not yet found it.

Shortly after we broke up, my ex-wife gave our son up for adoption. At the time I had a lot of excuses why I wouldn't fight for his custody, but the reality was that I was in no condition to raise a baby, especially alone. I often think of him. Where is my son today? How is he doing? Who did he grow up to be? And, most importantly, does he know Jesus Christ?

I had moved back home shortly after the divorce, and some time later I married again—the woman who, after twenty-three years, is still my wife.

I started drinking more heavily, smoking pot, sniffing speed, and as time went on, my bondage grew progressively worse. I no longer had a choice. It wasn't just that I didn't want to live without them. I *couldn't* live without them. In addition, I started to get caught breaking the law—drunk driving, fighting, stealing. As my life got worse, I neglected and abused my family, the most precious thing that I had on this earth.

**A Moment of Surrender.** Then one day in 1989, while I was serving a sentence for a drunk driving charge, I received a disturbing and painful phone call from my wife. She told me that she and our children didn't want me to come back home. They were going to move and would not give me their new address. I realized that I could no longer fight the Lord's calling. With the help of the prison chaplain, I surrendered my life to Jesus.

That night, something happened to me deep inside. There were no fireworks, no earth-shaking experiences, but something unique had happened. I was given new life, the new life that God gives to everyone he washes in his blood and regenerates by his Holy Spirit. I really felt like a changed man.

The chaplain could see the change in me and called my wife to ask her to give me one last chance. I thank God that she did. I don't blame my family for not wanting me back, because I was really messed up. Even though they loved me, they feared me more.

From that moment on, life was new and different. The things that I used to like a lot—booze, drugs, foul language, dirty books—I no longer enjoyed. In fact, I strongly disliked them. When problems came (and they still come), I knew that God was on my side helping and guiding me. I understood that all my struggles came when I tried to handle them on my own, instead of giving them to God and seeking his guidance.

Even though I am still in prison, God has led me and my family out of slavery and into a new freedom. We have three sons, one daughter, and four grandchildren. Life in prison is still a struggle. It can get very lonely, and temptation is all around. But every day, the Lord keeps softening my heart. I know he's with me, whatever I face. Besides, he's given me the family that I've always wanted and a place where I feel that I do fit in. What's more important, he's shown me that he has always been my Father, that Jesus has always been with me, and that the Holy Spirit is the best Counselor anyone can have. ■

# 5

# Gabby

**by Hazel Roeder**

When I began to write about my experiences with my daughter Gabby, my mind was flooded with memories. As I wrote, I came to see that each time I was at my wits' end—completely empty and needy—I met Jesus. We are so blessed, so undeservedly blessed!

**A Precious—And Challenging—Gift from God.** Gabby accepts her life as God has given it to her. Gabby is thirty-four years old, and her favorite things are *The Muppet Show*, nursery rhymes, infant musical toys, and playing "patty-cake." Her best friends are her "boss" and me. Gabby goes to "work" in the prevocational department of our county vocational training center. She is legally blind, profoundly retarded, unable to speak, and can only walk when assisted. Because her feet are malformed, she wears heavy braces from her laced-up shoes to her knees.

Gabby is the third of my six children, and while I had everyone else in my house functioning like clockwork, Gabby was always lagging behind. Since I was always an active and energetic person, I wasn't used to waiting. Throughout the early years of Gabby's life, I would lose my patience with her, particularly when I had a very full schedule. There were times when I got so frustrated that I would yell at her or even squeeze her arm. By God's grace, I knew she did not deserve my wrath, but I would get so frustrated by how much she needed me.

I went to confession often. I know God heard my cries for help, but it took quite a long time before I saw a deep breakthrough. The change came when my confessor told me to read the story of Saul's conversion in Acts 9 for my penance. I literally spent months reading this story, asking the Spirit to change my heart. Then I finally saw it. When Jesus said, "Saul, Saul, why do you persecute me?" (Acts 9:4), I knew that Jesus was saying those words to me. I recalled that Jesus had said at another time, "Whatever you do to the least of my brothers and sisters, you do to me" (Matthew 25:40). It was Jesus I was dealing with.

As I began to treat Gabby the way I hoped I would treat Jesus—with love, patience, kindness, and compassion—I began to understand that she was not a burden but God's gracious gift to me. Through her, I was humbled. I came to know the Lord, Gabby, and myself, in a deeper way. This was just the beginning of the change, however. There would be many opportunities to grow and learn more deeply how to love Gabby as if she were Jesus himself.

**Going Deeper.** When Gabby first came home to live with us full-time after spending thirteen years away at a special school, I tried to fit her into my life without cutting back on my duties or activities. Up to that point, she had only been with us on weekends, holidays and during the summer months. Having Gabby around all the time led to many tense moments that I tried to shrug off—until the day that she refused to come down the stairs. I had bathed and dressed her and needed to give her breakfast and send her off to work so that I could be on time for my weekly Bible study.

Normally, going down the stairs wasn't too hard for us. Gabby would hold onto the stair rail, and I would hold her arm on her other side, and we would walk down the stairs together. This particular morning, however, she became frightened—probably because she sensed my anxiety and need to hurry. I started tugging her. She became more frightened and would not budge. First, I cried. Then, I changed my tone and softly reassured her that I would help her. Carefully I nudged and prompted, but she still resisted. No amount of prompting or encouraging was going to move her, and time was ticking away. I got so upset with her, I didn't know what to do.

By God's grace, I realized what was happening. This Bible-toting mother was angry enough to be tempted to strike her innocent daughter in order to be on time for a Bible study! I sat her down in a safe place, grabbed a crucifix, and, weeping, fell on my knees as I poured out my heart to Jesus. I thanked him for taking my punishment on the cross so that at that very moment, I could repent, be forgiven, and sin no more. That was when I felt the Spirit filling my mind with the truth. I had always believed I was very gentle and incapable of violence. But the Spirit showed me how I thought I was better than others, and that it should be easy for me to take care of Gabby if I just tried hard enough.

I was humbled by what I saw—both my sin and the fact that God's love is stronger and capable of overcoming all evil. Jesus' death on the cross saved a sinner like me and granted me a life flowing from his resurrection. After God comforted me with his presence, I had a complete change of heart and mind. Whatever Gabby needed was my number one priority. If the best we could do all day was to sit on the stairs, I knew God would provide. Over the years, this understanding has grown. I learned to give each day to the Lord Jesus, trusting that he knew best what I could and could not do. He assured me that with his power and presence I could be a good wife and a good mother, but that I was not supposed to be a superwoman.

**A Deeper Love for Gabby.** About five years ago—Gabby was twenty-nine and I was fifty-six—Gabby began to lose her balance, and we both would fall. Once again, my response was anger. Her gait became increasingly unstable, and my anger would surface even if we were just stumbling. I knew that fear was behind the anger—fear that one of us was really going to get hurt.

When I asked the Lord to show me what was on my heart, he revealed what was hidden from my conscience: I was drawing the line with him again. I was angry at him because I was afraid that Gabby would become disabled and housebound, which would tie me down forever. When I realized what I was doing, I prayed God would change my heart so that I could agree to follow his will. I took her to the doctor hoping he could do something for her, but he couldn't. I knew, by absolute grace, that if Gabby and I were housebound, we would have every grace and blessing that we would ever need. Amazingly, after many months of working through this, the falling stopped!

There is so much more that I could write, but I feel I should end it here. There have been thirty-four years of struggle and growth I could describe, and every struggle has been a gracious gift from God. Gabby has always been a pure, gentle spirit, even when I have been tyrannical. I've written a lot about God's transforming work in my life, but the best is the change of heart God has worked in me. He's given me a deep love for Gabby. She is never a burden. She is not the neediest person I know. We are all the same when we stand before God—utterly needy and boundlessly loved. ■

# 6

# All Life Is Sacred

**by Mary Ann Henke**

Twenty years ago, my brother was murdered in New York. At the time, I was living in California with my husband and two young daughters, and we were joyfully anticipating the birth of our third child. Then, on a sunny Friday afternoon in September of 1975, my husband had the grim task of telling me that Andrew had been shot through the head and killed. Words cannot fully express what I felt—denial, uncontrollable weeping, a sense that part of me had died, a sense of being enveloped by darkness.

Andrew's death was like an instant blinding light from within. I experienced a "split-second" glimpse into the heart of Jesus. I understood, perhaps for the first time, that people are far more precious than any possession, power, or prestige that this world holds dear. The gift of life is sacred and of infinite value. Andy's absence made me realize that people are the crown of God's creation.

**A Conflict in My Conscience.** That very day, I went into labor and gave birth to our son. The emotional pendulum swung from the agony of death to the ecstasy of birth. After two more years in California, we moved back to New Jersey, and our fourth child, a daughter, was born. During this time, I watched my emotions change from anger to bitterness, then to rage, and finally to a desire for revenge. I kept reminding myself about my previous insight that life is precious and infinite and that people are to be valued over possessions. Of course I knew Andrew's life was precious, but did his killer deserve the same consideration? He took a life and he deserved to forfeit his. He deserved to die.

The conflict in my conscience bothered me. Our local parish had an appeal for CCD teachers, and I decided to volunteer. One of our teacher-education programs was to study in depth the American Bishops' Pastoral Letter on Peace entitled *The Challenge of Peace: God's Promise and Our Response*. We heatedly discussed nuclear war, social justice, and capital punishment. I remember getting so angry at another participant that I asked, "Did you ever have a family member senselessly murdered in cold blood? Let the police catch this killer and strap him into the electric chair. I'll pull the lever!" Yet, through all my anger and rage, I kept hearing a haunting voice: "Blessed are the peacemakers, for they shall be called the children of God" (Matthew 5:9).

I was very diligent and committed to CCD. I researched the Scriptures and drew up detailed lesson plans. Little did I know that at the same time our great Healer-God was softening my heart. Scripture study, a personal prayer life, and the Eucharist became a daily part of my life. What I kept hearing on a "heart level" was the recurrent theme of forgiveness. Jesus taught about it in the Sermon on the Mount. He prayed it in the "Our Father." He told Peter, in no uncertain terms, to forgive seventy times seven times.

And he lived it par excellence. As he hung on the cross, Jesus manifested his limitless love by forgiving and interceding on our behalf. He didn't succumb to hatred and revenge, but practiced what he preached. Herein lies the "triumph of the cross."

**"Am I a Hypocrite?"** In the early- to mid-1980s, my spiritual conversion intensified as I was drawn into the Catholic charismatic renewal. I attended a Life in the Spirit seminar and was prayed over for the release of the Holy Spirit so that I could personally experience the grace of Pentecost. The Holy Spirit, who was indwelling since my infant baptism, burst forth to give me the courage to proclaim beyond a shadow of a doubt that "Jesus is Lord!" I knew that the challenge now was that my thoughts, words, and actions must all flow from this faith-statement.

The time had finally come for me to to ask myself the question, "Am I truly a disciple of Jesus, or am I a hypocrite? How can I be an advocate of capital punishment after identifying so closely with Jesus and his teachings?" I knew that it went completely against my Christian conscience. Jesus gave us a new commandment, a new covenant sealed with his own blood: "Love one another as I have loved you." Am I just giving lip service to my faith in Jesus?

With the help of the Holy Spirit, a wise spiritual director, and much prayer, I came to the point where I could separate the sin from the sinner, the action from the person. The sin of murder is to be condemned, but the sinner is to be loved and forgiven. It is illogical to say that murder is wrong and then utilize the death penalty.

People will argue against capital punishment and say that there's always the possibility of executing an innocent person. Others will argue that the poor and uneducated are disproportionately executed compared to those from the privileged classes. Both arguments may be true, but neither one is my primary reason for opposition to the death penalty. Innocent or guilty, rich or poor, all life is sacred because God is the author of life and Jesus calls us to forgive.

**The Power to Forgive.** How can we carry out Jesus' mandate to forgive totally as he did? I can tell you from my own experience that, strictly speaking, it is impossible on a human level. It is only through God's grace and through the indwelling Holy Spirit that we can function as God functions. God is a God of love and forgiveness, mercy and compassion.

I have forgiven my brother's killer from my heart and have prayed for his salvation. Someday in eternity, it is my deep desire to hear the "voice" that haunted me so long ago say, "Come and join your risen brother Andrew." With great joy, I'll embrace him. But it will also give me great joy to embrace his killer as a brother and forgive him face to face.

I have arrived at the point where I can actually thank God for Andy's death. He was like the grain of wheat that died in order to produce an abundant harvest. I have told this story to others and I can tell by the expressions on their faces that they are thinking, "She must be crazy!" My consolation is that Jesus' family thought he was crazy too. But he was vindicated in the end, and by my baptism I share in his victory.

I wrote this story for a few reasons: First and foremost, to give glory to God. Second, to honor my brother's memory and to say that his life was not in vain. His death proved to be a turning point in my life. Third, in the hope that some part of my story will help another person enter more deeply into a loving relationship with God. Finally, every time I review my story, I experience deeper inner healing, and it sets my spirit free. All praise to Jesus, the Healer of my soul, my God and my all, my strength and my joy! ■

# 7

# Abba Father!

**by Bob Sheire**

In the past, there were two persons of the Trinity whom I loved and experienced and prayed to—the Son and the Holy Spirit. The Father, however, was always somewhere in the distance, a person I could not reach. I didn't feel I was worthy to reach him, nor did I believe that he had time for me. Within this last year, however, I have found that the Father is not only approachable, but that he longs for a relationship with his sons and daughters. We must learn to accept that and to return his love. We have to understand how real he is, how passionately in love he is with his creation, how deeply he wants to have a personal relationship with us. The Father doesn't need this relationship, but we need it, and he wants it.

The reasons for my emotional distance from my God the Father are deep-seated. You see, I never knew my biological father as I was growing up. He was a bank robber in Indiana, and he was arrested and put in prison when I was only one week old. My mother remarried and I was given my stepfather's name: Sheire. My stepfather was a hardworking man, but unfortunately, he was an alcoholic and abusive. Childhood for me was filled with many painful experiences of my stepfather; I never knew a father's love.

When I was about twenty years old, shortly after I got married, I saw my real father on television: he had become a Baptist missionary in South America. When I saw this preacher, I was amazed that he had the same name that I thought was my real name, Harold Robert Holflinger. Back in those days, television was live, so I called the station and asked to speak to the minister. He was still there, and I asked him, "Do you have two sons by the name of Louis and Bob?" There was a long silence. Then he asked me who I was. I said, "I'm Bob." He answered, "Well, I'm your father."

**Searching for Fatherly Love.** I met with my real father a couple of times, but didn't actively pursue a relationship with him because my stepfather was still alive. As bad as that relationship was, I felt a loyalty to him because he had put a roof over my head and food on the table. But after my stepfather died, I began to see my biological father on a regular basis. We were able to establish a good relationship, but the anger and pain about his having abandoned me still remained. Fatherly love still seemed to be eluding me.

As my wife and I grew in our relationship, I became a father myself—in fact, the father of eight children over the next twelve years. I always tried to be a good father, and I grew closer to the church—but there was a void in my life. Because I had never known a father's love, it was difficult for me to love my children. Looking back now, I can see the many times when I failed my children. Even so, the Lord was watching over them because they have all grown up to be fine adults.

As the children got older, my wife and I had more time to seek the wonderful things that the church had to offer. About a year ago, a number of my friends attended a conference that focused on the Father's love. I was not able to go, but I asked them to bring back tapes of the talks so I could listen and pray about what I heard. As I spent time with those tapes, praying and studying Scripture, I asked the Father to reveal to me how much he loved me, because I desperately needed to know the love of a father. During one particular time of prayer, God did reveal his deep love for me; it was probably the most wonderful experience of my sixty-three years of life. I came to understand how wonderfully the Father loved me, how much he cared for me—even that he was my Daddy. I felt that I was being cradled in his arms, sitting on his lap like a beloved child. I felt as if all of the fatherly love that had been denied me over the years was poured into me in a few hours' time.

**Running into Our Father's Arms.** When we are small children, we run eagerly to our daddies. What joy we feel as we are received by them! They raise us up, lift us high, and bounce us on their knees. That is what I experienced with my heavenly Father. It was simply acceptance—what I had always wanted from a father and very seldom received. Many of us have experienced times when we needed our fathers but they were not there for us, perhaps through no fault of their own. I've never experienced that loss with my heavenly Father; his love is constant. Over this past year, whenever I have felt unhappy, I turn to him and he pours out his mercies and blessings.

In my case—and I'm sure I'm not alone in this—my relationships with my father and my stepfather were so flawed that I looked at God the Father in fear. I was unsure that he was capable of giving me any more love than they had. Praise God, the Father has no flaws in his love. There are no strings attached. His love is unconditional. He says: "I love you; I created you; my Son Jesus died for you; our relationship is secure." And that is the difference.

I can now see that my fatherly love for my children was often conditional. I loved them more when they were good than I did when they were not good, more when they obeyed than when they disobeyed. My children are now in their thirties and forties, but it's not too late. I am trying to reflect the compassionate love of the Father to my children, to have more compassion for them. I hope that, in time, this will enable them to experience the Father's love as I have experienced it.

I have forgiven my biological father and I have also forgiven my stepfather. But this could not happen until I had come to know my heavenly Father's love. I hold no anger toward either man. I can't hold anger against anybody, because the Father holds no anger against me. During my initial experience of coming to know the Father's love, I felt him reassuring me that I would never be angry with anyone again. Even though I can be very hotheaded at times, since that time a year ago, I have not been angry with anyone. God healed me tremendously in that regard.

I've always known that Jesus loved me because he died on the cross for me; he poured out his precious blood for me. I've understood that, and I've experienced the presence of Jesus in my life. Yet when I asked the Father to come into my life, it was an even greater experience. Jesus is the Father's Son, and I am the Father's son. I am a brother to Jesus, and that same love and compassion that the Father has for his Son Jesus, he has for me. It's hard to comprehend that with all the billions of people in the world, the Father is so intimately in love with each and every one of us. But we have to understand that this is the nature of our Father's heart. ■

# 8

# Practicing What I Preach

**by John Libby**

I'm a "cradle Catholic." There was always a Bible in my home, but it was one of those three-hundred dollar Bibles that was opened only for births, deaths, and marriages. I had been an altar boy and even was a lector, up until I was arrested for my crime.

I was into drugs and illicit sex. But I still considered myself "religious." I now know my religion was mostly for show, not for real.

A couple of days before my sentencing, while still out on bail, I called the county jail and asked what reading materials I could bring in when I started my sentence. They said I could bring in a paperback Bible. I've always been a reader. If I didn't have anything to read, I'd write something just so I could read it. So I went and got an inexpensive paperback Catholic Bible and went to jail.

**Reading the Bible.** After "settling in," I pulled out the Bible and started reading, beginning on page one. I approached it like any other book I'd read: for entertainment. And it *was* entertaining—Genesis and Exodus had some exciting stories, Leviticus and Deuteronomy with their Jewish laws that I'm glad we Catholics don't have to follow, the histories of the other books of the Old Testament—it was all interesting and "entertaining." I kept reading. I finally got to the Book of Psalms and decided to skip it. Who wants to read a bunch of dry, old prayers? I'm reading for entertainment, remember?

About the time I was finished with the Book of Daniel, I was transferred from the San Antonio County Jail to the Garza unit of the Texas state prison system. There I encountered my first prayer circle. Well, I was "religious," so I joined. The meetings consisted of a testimony about God working in someone's life, petitions, and then ended with the "Our Father." Afterwards, while being welcomed by the members of the prayer circle, "something" (someone?) *made* me volunteer, out of the blue, to provide a Bible reading for each prayer circle meeting. The idea was enthusiastically accepted by the members of the prayer circle.

**Discovering the Psalms.** As I went back to my bunk that night, I questioned myself. Why in the world did I volunteer to do that? How am I going to pick out something for a *prayer* circle out of the Bible? *Where* can I find something for the *prayer* circle? The word *prayer* kept standing out in my mind. Prayers? Psalms! Okay, I'll go check out the Book of Psalms. It's a collection of prayers, right? So I went back and started reading the Book of Psalms. Wow! How could I have skipped them before? I discovered a God who is merciful, loving, and forgiving, and who only "lowered the boom" on his people when they started adoring other gods.

Two years later, I was switched to another unit, and I started a new prayer circle in my dorm. I still read a short passage from the Bible and preach about the passage at each prayer circle nightly gathering. About eight to fifteen inmates attend out of up to sixty-eight in the dorm. I had been doing this for about nine months when it happened: the "test."

**The Prison Culture.** I haven't mentioned the "culture and customs" of prison life. Mostly it is calm and apparently peaceful. But just under the surface are frustration, loneliness and—always waiting to erupt—violence.

I came back from chow one day and someone had broken into my locker and stolen about forty dollars' worth of food and hygiene products. I was angry. I was hurt that these people I "trusted" would do this. I wondered why God, who had protected me so far, would let this happen. Well, as long as I didn't know who did it, I could be angry but not have to do anything. By evening, I had pretty much gotten over it.

The next day, three people came to me, at different times, to tell me who had broken into my locker. Yes, beyond a doubt, this person *had* done it. Now prison "culture and customs" came into play. I was expected to "take care of business." To "protect myself," I was expected to beat him up. This violence was to show that nobody could steal *my* stuff and get away with it. Telling the guards was out. TDC (Texas Department of Corrections) to some of us means "They Don't Care." And that could cause more trouble because I would be labeled a snitch. No, I was expected to handle this myself.

**Forgiving the Thief.** And I *wanted* to beat him up. I wanted to smash his face in. I wanted to kick his ribs in, and break his arms. But I'd been preaching from the

Bible to these inmates for nine months. What to do? I prayed about it. Fight? Protect my "stuff"? Forgive? Let it happen again because I'm "weak"?

I don't consider myself weak. But I truly believe what I read and preach in the Bible. I could forgive the thief and possibly be thought of as weak, or I could be a hypocrite, and fight. I don't *think* I'm weak, but I *know* I'm not a hypocrite. That was my answer.

So I went to the different gang leaders and explained that I was going to forgive the thief, that I believed in the Bible and what Jesus said. Then I confronted the thief publicly. "I know you stole my stuff. But I forgive you. Why did you do it? I thought I could trust you." He mumbled that he hadn't done it, that I could check his locker. But he couldn't look me in the eye, and he actually ran off. I didn't ask him to return my stuff; Luke 6:30 says, "And from the one who takes from you do not demand it back."

After he ran off, I realized I should have been scared. He was young and very muscular. And I was publicly calling him a thief, something frowned upon even in prison. I should have been scared, but I wasn't. Later, the gang leaders came to me and said that they saw my point. They said I no longer needed a lock on my locker. From now on, my "stuff" was safe. Nobody would take anything from me again.

**A Friend of God.** I had passed a "heart check"! They now knew I believed what I preached. And God had protected me: by my following what he taught, I was safe in his hands. The Bible has been my shield and Jesus has been my salvation.

Since my sentencing, I have been happier and more at peace than in the ten years before I got locked up. Don't get me wrong—I want to get out of jail! But I know I can live my religion now, and I know what it is to *be* religious. What I was before was for show.

I am currently three years into a twelve-year "aggravated" sentence. I come up for parole in another three years. I hope to get into prison ministry when I do get out. I know my life and beliefs have changed dramatically for the better and my life will be much different than it used to be. God used my jail sentence to turn an evil into a good—for me to truly be his friend, as he truly is mine. ■

9

# There's Always Time to Save a Soul

**by Marion Foca**

Three years ago, my husband was hospitalized at Westchester County Medical Center in Valhalla, New York. His roommate, Jim, was a man in his early forties who appeared very gaunt and was in poor health. When I introduced myself to him, he explained that his body was destroyed by alcohol.

He never had any visitors, and I began to feel a great deal of compassion for him. After my husband left the hospital, I continued to visit Jim, and often my husband came with me.

I tried to provide my new friend with whatever comforts I could, and I soon found myself wondering if Jim was at peace with God. I eventually found the courage to ask him if he was brought up in any religion. He explained to me that his mother had been an alcoholic and that there was no religion in his upbringing.

As Jim's condition worsened, I was obsessed with wanting to bring him to know God. I prayed to the Holy Spirit to help me find the words. One day, I asked him if he believed in God. Jim said it was very difficult for him to believe in something he could not see.

We also cannot see the wind, I explained to him, but we know it's there because of what it can do. Following along that same line of thought, we must believe God is here because of what he can do. God knew Jim needed a friend, and the Lord had chosen my husband and me for him. I always ended my visits by telling him I was praying for him, and he accepted this with a smile.

Jim's condition grew worse, and I finally asked him if he would like to be baptized. To my delight, he said he would like that very much. I brought a priest to the hospital, and after they had a long conversation, Jim was baptized, and I became his godmother. I felt the weight of the world lifted off my shoulders.

That same evening, Jim was rushed into the hospital's intensive care unit, where a tracheotomy was performed. He was unable to speak after that, but he would communicate with me by writing simple notes.

Weeks passed. My visits regularly ended with a prayer, and Jim would hang on to every word. He wrote me notes saying that a priest from the hospital was giving him Holy Communion, and that delighted me. As the weeks flew by, he became weaker. Finally, seven months after I first met him, Jim began to slip into a coma. The priest who baptized him visited him one last time and anointed him.

Jim passed away four hours later and entered the kingdom of heaven. The idea of a "deathbed conversion" causes some to be doubtful of the authenticity of the convert's intentions, but Jesus knows when someone turns to him in genuine faith—even at the last minute.

Read Luke 23:32-43, which ends, "And he said to Jesus, 'Lord remember me when you come into your kingdom.' And Jesus said to him, 'Amen I say to you, today you shall be with me in Paradise.' " ■

# 10

# Love Is the Answer

**by Kay G.**

Today, something wonderful happened to me that I would like to share with you. About ten years ago, when I was doing some volunteer work at a home for wayward girls, I met a young girl named Annette. She was a drug addict and had turned to prostitution to keep up her habit. She was eighteen years old and was about to be released from the home. With nowhere else to go, she asked if I would take her in.

My husband and I had raised eight children—all of whom graduated from college. My husband had passed away in 1977, and when all the children married, I found myself alone most of the time, so I bought a smaller home. I wasn't sure I wanted all the responsibility. Still, I felt that the Lord was telling me to agree to take Annette in. I suspected she might be a handful to manage, but I couldn't get away from the sense of God's calling for me.

I had led a pretty sheltered life up until that point, but as I got more involved with Annette, I learned what a drug-related life involved. If my children knew where my commitment to this girl would lead me—visiting her in a dingy motel or driving down a street infested with drug houses—I'm sure they would have committed me to an insane asylum!

**Love Is the Answer.** One thing my husband and I always insisted on with our children was respect. Annette had no concept of this, and this was the hardest thing for me to cope with. She could be rude, demanding, and dishonest. It was common for her to take twenty dollars from my purse and apologize later. She was arrested for soliciting three times, and each time I had to go pay bail for her. Many times, I told God I couldn't take any more. But he would always say, "Love is the answer."

Many times I wanted to give up on Annette. We would quarrel often about her lifestyle or about the expectations she would place on me, but she would always say that she'd be "six feet under" if it weren't for me. I was the only person in the world who cared about her. I prayed many rosaries for Annette—and for myself, asking God to give me the grace to see this through. Always, the same thought would come to my mind: "Love is the answer."

A few years ago, Annette got into a fight and received a blow to her head that affected her mentally. Combined with her drug habit and her inability to take care of herself, this wound left her even more unstable than before. Because of her disability, she now receives financial help from the government, and this has enabled her to live on her own—but it's not always the best thing for her.

**Learning to Act with Kindness.** Recently, Annette was released from another jail term and has since managed to have a few months free from drugs. Today, however, I realized that she had taken five dollars from my wallet. She was short on cash and had to wait a week or so for her next check. When I realized it was gone, I became furious. I began to think she was getting back into her old habits. But this time, I decided to handle the situation differently. I decided to be really kind. I let her know that I realized the money was missing, but I didn't accuse her.

When Annette saw that I didn't react angrily or get into another argument, her heart softened. She asked me to forgive her and told me that she really appreciates everything I've done for her. Hearing Annette speak so honestly and gratefully touched my heart deeply, and I learned something very important.

Through all the years that Annette was in my life, we argued whenever she did something I thought was inappropriate. When I decided to show kindness instead of anger, the Lord showed me that—what with the blow Annette had received to her head, the drugs she had taken, and her very difficult childhood—love was what she needed most of all. I realized too that I had asked God to forgive me many times, and he did.

I had spent so many years judging and being impatient with people—even my own children. But today, I realized that God was trying to tell me all the time, "Love is the answer." I feel now that I finally know what he means. If we want to know what happiness is, all we have to do is try to show some kindness to the people we meet. I heard it said once, "It is better to be kind than to be right." I'm praying that I will be able to live this motto all the days of my life. ∎

# 11

# If You Believe, You Will See the Glory of God

### by Tommy Skaggs

I appreciate this opportunity to tell you what God is doing in my life. Although this makes me feel a bit uncomfortable, I know that when I'm uncomfortable, I'm growing. And that is what I need to be doing all the time—growing—because for so long I was dormant and dead.

I was born and raised in Baltimore, Maryland. I had a wonderful mother, a good father, and never really wanted for anything as a kid. As I grew up, I started smoking a little bit of weed, popping some pills, and drinking from time to time. But I was still able to function and work and prosper. I even had an opportunity to start working for a bank. I liked working with numbers, and I had an opportunity to meet many people. Even though all the time I was smoking weed, drinking, and popping pills, I still managed to function and even excel at my job. Eventually, I became an officer for the bank. I was running one of their offices, had a wonderful wife, and three beautiful sons.

**Filling the Void.** Even though everything seemed to be going well and I was living the American dream, still something was missing. I was still using the drugs, trying to find out what was missing. I started smoking cocaine, and that is from

Satan. I started having problems with money. I didn't think the problem was with drugs, but with money. If I could just get more money, I thought, I would be okay. So I forgot whose money I was working with. I thought that it was my money, and I started taking it. Initially, I thought I would take a little bit of money to pay the drug dealer, and then everything would be okay. But when I handed him the money, he had another bag of dope there for me. Being a drug addict, I couldn't say, "No, I'm okay, I don't need it." I *had* to take it.

In the end, everything just snowballed. Here I am, working at this bank, in this office, and every time the phone rings, I don't know if it will be the auditors or security. Yet at the same time, I couldn't stop smoking the cocaine. Eventually, I just figured I couldn't keep going to work anymore because I couldn't stop picking up the money. I felt terrible about it.

I quit my job and in a very short time, since I wasn't there to cover up my tracks, I had detectives looking for me. I decided to confess and hoped the courts would force me to get clean. When I went to court, the judge gave me ten years. He waited a couple of minutes, and after I sat there and cried and fell on the floor, he suspended my sentence and gave me five years of probation, alternative sentencing, and drug counseling. I was happy because I thought I wouldn't be able to get high anymore. That was a lie. I even violated probation.

**In the Mire.** My wife, who loved me more than anything in the world, finally said, "You've got to go." By this time I wasn't just doing cocaine in the evenings. I needed something to bring me down and I started shooting heroin. Now I was a heroin addict *and* a cocaine addict. I started stealing from my family. I stole from my wife, my children, my sister-in-law. I was out on the streets, sleeping under bridges, in old houses or parks—any place I could find. My brother had said something about my feet being in the mire and in the clay. I was up to my neck in it. But I tried everything—hospitals, jails—and I just couldn't stop.

Finally on December 28, 1998, a man by the name of Scott decided to let me come into Beacon House, a ministry for homeless men and drug addicts. I had to crawl in that front door. I was so beat up, I think I weighed only 130 pounds. They put me in detox, and I couldn't move for three days. I remember that on Friday, I was sitting down there in detox, and I heard this music, beautiful music. I crawled up the steps and realized that they were having a worship service. They were singing about Jesus and praising him. It seemed like it was magic or something. When the music stopped, a man went to a microphone and started talking about what Jesus was doing for them.

I will never forget this one guy, Nick, with tattoos all over his body, looking big and mean. He stepped up to the microphone and when he talked about Jesus, tears started coming down his face. I thought to myself—if Jesus can do this for him, he could do something for me.

**Coming Out of the Tomb.** When the pastor got up, he started to read from the Gospel of John about the raising of Lazarus. When Jesus said, "Take away the stone," Martha, the sister of the dead man, warned that there would be a bad odor. Jesus said, "Did I not tell you that if you believed, you would see the glory of God?" Then Jesus called in a loud voice, "Lazarus, come out." The dead man came out, his hands and feet wrapped with strips of linen and a cloth around his face. Jesus said to them, "Take off the grave clothes and let him go" (John 11:38-44).

This passage spoke to me so much. I had been dead. I *was* dead. I had been in that tomb far longer than four days and I was stinking. I was stinking badly, with sin of every kind. And Jesus said, "Take off the grave clothes and let him go." The pastor said, "That is you." I didn't hear Jesus talking to *Lazarus* to come out. It was just like he was talking to *me*: "Tommy, come out. Tommy, come out." These guys had already rolled away the stone for me. Jesus called me out of the tomb. He took off all of my dead clothes. I wasn't stinking anymore and he began to clothe me in something else—his righteousness.

Romans 10:9-10 talks about "confessing with your mouth and believing with your heart." That is the important thing, believing with your heart. A man named Joe talked to me about believing. He said, "We addicts have always believed in something we could see, whether it was the drug dealer on the corner or that package of dope. But now it is time to believe in something you can't see." I held on to that, and I said, "I am going to believe, I am going to believe." I've believed in everything else and it failed me. Nothing could satisfy me. So I am going to believe in something that I can't see. "Believe and you will see the glory of God." I knew that the change had to take place in my heart. Change what is going on in your heart, and you are going to change the way you think. Change the way you think, and you are going to change the way you behave.

**God Doesn't Make Mistakes.** So that is what I did. God is such an awesome God. He is a God of reconciliation and restoration, so much so that he decided to send his Son, his one and only Son. I have three beautiful boys whom I love with all my heart. I would lay down my life for them in a minute, but I would never sacrifice their lives. Yet that's what the Father did. Yes, I made a lot of mistakes, but you know what? I am not a mistake. God doesn't make mistakes. He said, "Tommy, I'm going to fix you." I said, "You know what? I believe you, Lord. I believe you." I've seen him working. He put me in a place where I could see. I am so blessed. Then he started restoring my relationship with my wife, and started bringing people back into my life that I had lost—or thought I had lost.

So guess what? I started to believe and guess what I started to see? The glory of God! That is what it is. If you don't believe, you are not going to see the glory. It is going to pass you right by. And I see this glory—God has put me in a place where I can't miss it. I've seen him healing other men and doing wonderful things in their lives.

My message is to believe, and you will see the glory of God. Change your heart, then your mind will change and your behavior will change. God has delivered me from so much and blessed me in so many ways. He has blessed me through the people he has put in my life. I just praise and glorify you, Lord, and give you all the glory. I thank you for giving me a heart of believing, so that I can see your glory. ■

# 12

# Out of Bondage

### by Katie A. Gesto

I was always the "good" kid—not even because I was trying, but just because that's the way I was. I loved going to Mass and confession, and grew up with a desire to help people in some way. Mom called me "Sunshine" because I was always so cheery. I tried hard not to cause my parents any trouble.

In the years that followed, my sunny personality began to cloud. Family conflicts, insecurities that go along with adolescence, hatred of being overweight—even though I was quite thin—and a lack of a solid identity, all contributed to this. I bottled up every feeling, but outwardly kept on smiling. Playing sports was my main outlet of emotions and energy.

All of these factors were a ripe medium for the onset of bulimia when I turned fifteen. At that time, I had never heard of anyone with bulimia, and basically fell into it by trying to make myself sick after a Thanksgiving meal. I found that it was a seemingly wonderful way to stay thin for sports while having the pleasure of eating sweets. Little did I know how that decision would change the course of my life. Quickly I was swept away by the fierceness of the addiction.

**Keeping Secrets**. I did a great job of keeping the problem a secret from my family and friends. It's a wonder how sneaky I became. I could shovel in half a loaf of bread and butter with a half a gallon of ice-cream in about five minutes while "cleaning up the dishes" alone after family meals. This was followed by purging episodes of up to eight times each day. I particularly feared making my habit public, because I was being recruited for a volleyball scholarship by a number of universities. My chances would be shot if anyone found out.

Yet keeping the secret had its costs. I was growing more depressed, and hated the sneaky, shameful person I was becoming. I knew God was the answer and often sat in the church alone with Jesus in the Blessed Sacrament, begging him to help me stop. I knew he was behind the cure, but didn't know if I had the ability to wait for it. One evening while driving home from high school, I seriously thought of driving off the ramp to end my life.

I received a full scholarship while maintaining the secret and I thought the new change of environment would bring my long-desired relief. To my grave disappointment, it only increased the incidence of episodes. I knew I didn't have the power to change as I had tried so many times before. A constant mental dialogue of self-condemnation and self-hatred made it difficult to focus, affecting my ability to play volleyball. My insecurity and self-loathing festered.

**Christ at the Center.** A hunger for something—or someone—to save me from my self-destruction spurred me on. At a Christian gathering during my university freshman year, I came to a deeper place in my relationship with God—one that would change the course of my recovery, and of my whole life. During that meeting, I heard for the first time that God wanted to be intimately and passionately involved with everything in my life, in such a way that I could be totally transformed, and freed of the grips of such addictions as bulimia. Could it be true?

There, hidden in the back of the room, I prayed a prayer of acceptance for Jesus to be the center of my life—a prayer acknowledging that he had the power to free me, and inviting the Holy Spirit to direct and heal my life, instead of myself. My life changed. I no longer felt that deep, searing emptiness that I had come to think was normal, or the hopelessness that I could never overcome this. A peace that superseded any peace I had known began filling my heart. I thought, "By next week I'll be back to normal, freed of bulimia!" And for a week I was okay—until it returned with a vengeance.

But even though the symptoms continued, I began understanding more of the causes of the eating disorder. Perfectionism and my poor self-image had to be confronted and changed by the power of the Holy Spirit. I had to stop hating myself for not living a radically high standard of perfection. I clung to a hope that one day I would be set free to live the vocation I believed God was calling me to—missionary work. I knew that if I were not totally healed, I would fall apart on the mission field.

Despite the great growth in love for God and inner healing during the next two years at the university, the bulimic habits still persisted; in fact they got worse. During my junior year of college, I was captain of the team, and had just returned from a wonderful missions conference, but to everyone's surprise, my secret seven-year bout with the monster became public. I became so incapacitated, unable to concentrate on my studies, or play volleyball, that I knew I needed to be hospitalized. This decision resulted in the forfeit of my scholarship and a long stay in an eating disorder hospital to learn to deal with the deadly issues fueling the addiction.

My hopes of not being a wound in my parents' hearts were shattered as they picked me up from the airport to drive me to the hospital. We were all silent. What was ahead for us? For me? Would this really cure me? Could God fully heal me? I believed he could but didn't know why he was taking so long.

My suppressed feelings began reawakening in the hospital. It had been over a decade since I had ever cried tears, but I made up for all those years as I experienced buried pain and wounding. Through the pain, I worked through my lack of trust in God, which was based in a wrong perception of his character. Little by little, I came to believe that he really did passionately love me—*all of me*—even when I had my head buried in the toilet. These new revelations of his love healed my heart and allowed me to love myself and reshape my thinking.

**A Gentle Healer.** One day, when I was feeling depressed and alone, I felt God speak to me in the quietness of my heart. God seemed to be saying: *Let me show you, let me reveal to you who you really are. You are my joy! Little one, don't be afraid to draw near, even though you feel filled with darkness, bitterness, and anger. Draw near. Only I can relieve* *the pain in your heart. It takes time, but trust me, your gentle healer. I love you!*

Two years after leaving the hospital, I returned to college to finish my nursing degree at the Franciscan University of Steubenville in Ohio. It was there that I decided to consecrate my life to the Blessed Virgin Mary. After that, I never again experienced that same compulsion and drive toward the bulimic habits. Through Christian counseling, friends praying with me, and precious time spent before Jesus in the Blessed Sacrament, the damaged parts of myself continue to be restored. The healing took eight years but through it, the Lord taught me so much.

God is true to his promises. He gave me a desire to serve him in the missions, and he has allowed me to fulfill that desire. While serving in Sudan for two years, we were bombed twice, I was sick with a number of tropical diseases, and I was very far from home when both my grandmothers died. Many other incidents happened while in other countries, but the force of bulimia never returned—even though I had been told that I would probably suffer relapses all my life when under stress. That is a miracle! Complete healing from an eating disorder and any addiction or difficulty *is* possible, thanks to the healing power of God's great love. I never thought I could be as happy and peaceful as I am today. Sometimes I remember where I was and look where I am now, and say, "Wow! You are an amazing God!" ■

# 13

# The Return of My Prodigal Son

**by Angie Shepherd**

The story of the prodigal son had always intrigued and perplexed me. Over the years, I heard numerous homilies explaining the story's complexities. In my carefree years and as a young mother, I could not comprehend the intricate meaning behind the written words. Little did I know that this story would become my legacy.

My husband Sam and I have a marriage blessed in heaven. I knew this from the very beginning, and within the course of five years, God gave us two beautiful sons. The early years were happy ones filled with baptisms, birthdays, wrestling matches, and baseball games. I tried to include God in my daily activities, and to instill this life-long friendship with God in my children too.

The teenage years can be a challenging experience for many parents, and we were no exception. The signs were subtle at first, and we dismissed them as "typical" teenage patterns of growing up. As one year, then two, then three, ticked away, the signs of drug abuse and rebellion in our older son crashed in on us like a mighty asteroid careening out of control. We were becoming accustomed to arriving home, after a social night with friends, to find the police waiting at our door.

Within three years, what we had saved for our boys' education was nearly depleted with legal fees and family counseling. During these years, my husband and I prayed that our son would be set free from his drug addiction. We experienced anger and embarrassment at his deterioration. We wondered if God had abandoned us.

**The Father's Unconditional Love.** During this time, I came across a book by Henri J. M. Nouwen entitled *The Return of the Prodigal Son, A Story of Homecoming*. Immediately I was drawn to learning more about this parable, because now I was in the midst of living it. I was especially moved by the title, stressing "The Return." I read this book over and over, each time gaining more insight about the Father's unconditional love toward both sons. I knew that loving my son was not an option, and I knew too that God's love for my son was greater than my own.

Finally, our son was arrested and sent to a prison facility five hours away. My worst fear had become a reality. I knew that I could not get through this experience without God's help. From reading the book about the prodigal son, I had learned many things about myself as well as about my son. Whenever I sin, am I not just like the wayward son who "leaves home to dwell in a distant country"? (Luke 15:13). Whenever I refuse to forgive another, do I resemble the elder son with my resentful attitude? As Nouwen states so perfectly, "Not only did the younger son, who left home to look for freedom and happiness in a distant country, get lost, but the one who stayed home also became a lost man" (p. 69).

More and more I was realizing God's unconditional love for my family. Friends began asking my husband and me how we could continue loving and forgiving our son after countless displays of foolish behavior. Our response time and again was always the same: "It's like an analogy of God's love for us. God never withdraws his love from us. We cannot explain it. Love is not optional." As Jesus commands, "Love God with your whole heart. . . . Love your neighbor as you love yourself" (Matthew 22:37,39).

**Taking Refuge in God.** I often read Psalm 91, which brought me comfort and a gratitude to God. I visualized my imprisoned son under God's protection: "With his pinions he will cover you, and under his wings you shall take refuge" (Psalm 91:4). I learned to depend on the Almighty for everything.

Each morning in my daily devotional time, I would imagine releasing my son from my narrow expectations into God's perfect design. With my inner sight, I would release him as one gently releases a feather from one's grasp. The release is ever so delicate, and the final destination can never be predetermined. I began to know, without a doubt, that the Father was in control of my family's situation. The results were in his hands. This conviction became so strong that I knew it was the work of the Holy Spirit. A deep peace filled my family and me.

When one is in the midst of chaos—whether it be a life-threatening illness, loss of a job or family member, divorce, or mental illness—it's time to step back and realize the preciousness of one's life. It is a time to reconnect with the Lord and remember from where and from whom we came.

Always, without exception, each experience holds a gift, although it may take years to find and unwrap.

**The Ability to Forgive.** My son's prison experience was, without a doubt, the beginning of his "return." By now, I was reading *The Return of the Prodigal Son* nightly. I kept reading about the Father's forgiveness and love. God was calling me to imitate these qualities. Forgiveness gradually became easier. The resentment, which had previously held me like a baited fishhook, slowly released its grip on my heart.

Two years ago, my husband gave me a print of Rembrandt's famous painting, *The Return of the Prodigal Son*, for Christmas. It was the perfect gift since it was also the first time in a year that my prodigal son returned home. Just like the parable, he was moved to repentance and became totally free from the grip of drugs. Just like the parable, I was able to forgive as the Father so lovingly forgives.

God's ultimate plan for our lives is rarely what we envision it to be. It is always greater. It is now three years since that fateful day of my son's arrest. God's glory has indeed been manifested. My son follows a twelve-step program, attends church, participates in a weekly Bible study, volunteers in a prison ministry, and spends time in adoration before the Blessed Sacrament.

I continue to thank God for the revelation of his love for all of us in the simple and ageless story of "The Prodigal Son." ■

# 14

# Changing Hatred into Love

### by Ann Washington

My story begins many years ago, when my husband and I separated. There were five children at home and I was two months pregnant with yet another. It was several years before I saw my husband again, and when I did, the very sight of him made me sick to my stomach.

The children saw their father from time to time, and whenever they would talk about him, the hatred in me would surface again, along with the knowledge that I had the responsibility of raising our children alone after he had married another woman. My hatred for this woman was so intense that I would lie awake at night plotting and fantasizing both of their deaths. At one point, I went so far as to buy a gun. Such hatred drove me to drink and led me down a path littered with sin.

As time went on, I became more dependent on alcohol. My life was being lost to the corrupt ways of this world. I couldn't seem to find fulfillment in anything I did. Through a series of divinely appointed circumstances, however, I began to go back to church to find peace. In a very short time, I committed myself to Jesus and began to see real changes in my life.

**Asking for Forgiveness.** I had sustained a deep hatred for my husband for more than twenty years. Now that I had turned my life over to Jesus, I knew that I needed to ask my husband to forgive me. I explained to him how Jesus had filled me with his Holy Spirit, how he had freed me and made me whole. For the first time in my life, I was able to forgive and love. I'll never forget the smile that came over his face and how he grabbed me and lifted me into the air with joy. However, even though he had separated from the other woman, I still wasn't sure if my forgiveness could extend to her.

Several weeks after that encounter, I had a dream that my husband was dying from cancer. I kept that dream in the back of my mind for a whole year. Then, one day, when I came home from work, my youngest son told me, "Daddy is in the hospital. Someone called and left this telephone number for you to call him right away." I replied, "For what? He wasn't at the hospital when I had you. Why should he call me for help after twenty-two years?"

Hours passed and I still hadn't returned the call. Then I felt the power of God move me as I recalled Jesus' words from the Gospel of Luke to love our enemies (Luke 6:27-35). As tears streamed down my face, I knew that my love for God and his desire for me to forgive my enemies was stronger than my desire for revenge. I had no other choice but to obey, so I called the hospital. When I visited him, however, he couldn't talk clearly, so I promised to come again the next day.

**The Armor of God.** That evening, I had a vision that my husband had cancer. It was at that moment that I realized the meaning of my dream a year earlier. I prayed to our heavenly Father to give me the guidance that I would need for my pending hospital visit. As I prayed, I saw a woman with children at the hospital, and I knew that God was preparing me for the fact that I would be coming face to face with the other family. In my heart, I still hated this woman, and I prayed for the strength of the Holy Spirit to help me handle this situation. I called out for the whole armor of God and sought the protection of the word of God. Satan may have wanted to see me lose, but God was providing me with his word so that I could win.

When I arrived at the hospital, the other family was entering the room at the same time. I walked over to this woman, for whom I had harbored hatred for all these years, and offered her my hand in peace. I was able to talk to her with no animosity in my heart.

Still, when my husband asked me to return to the hospital on a daily basis, I flatly refused. But when I arrived home and reviewed my actions at the hospital, I realized I still had a battle to fight. The devil was trying to persuade me to continue to seek revenge, and I could see how easy it would be for me because of my vulnerability. However, I kept my eyes on Jesus and decided to return to the hospital. I prayed with my husband prior to his surgery, that the word of God would take root in him, and I asked God to help me stand by this man and not give up on him.

A friend went with me to the hospital the next day, and the doctor informed me that my husband's cancer had become so advanced that it had spread to his liver. I knew what I needed to do. The three of us, while holding hands, prayed for physical and spiritual healing. I assured him that there was nothing to fear, that God would forgive him and love him no matter what.

**Praising God in All Things.** The following week, when I went to visit my husband, he was in such pain that I could hear his anguish and suffering out in the corridor. Guided by the Holy Spirit, I entered his room with a sign of peace. As I approached him, I laid my hand on his shoulder—his back was toward me—and he immediately turned over and started to talk. I then put one finger over his mouth and began to pray. He started to smile and his face glowed with happiness. He praised and thanked God as we continued to talk that evening for hours.

As the next three weeks passed, he didn't seem to have any complaints or pain. During the fourth week, however, he took a turn for the worse. Guided by the Holy Spirit, I prayed with him. He opened his eyes, smiled up at me, and stretched out his hand. All at once, he started shouting, "Praise the Lord, Praise the Lord, Praise the Lord!" These were the last words he spoke, to me or to anyone else. Two days later, he passed away.

Since that time, I have experienced a far deeper trust in Jesus. He gave me the strength to forgive my enemies. When you obey God's commandments to love and forgive, you end up receiving so much peace yourself. God stands behind his word, the word which Jesus spoke: "Pardon, and you shall be pardoned. Give, and it shall be given to you. Good measure pressed down, shaken together, running over, will they pour into the fold of your garment" (Luke 6:37-38). In forgiving others, I was able to forgive myself for having hated so much. "For the measure you measure with will be measured back to you" (6:38). ■

# 15

# Christmas in Jail

**by Lou T.**

When the Mexican teenager walked into the county jail, he was understandably nervous.

The nineteen-year-old, baby-faced Hispanic youth had never been in jail before and he had no idea what to expect. Would he be robbed, assaulted, raped? The other prisoners looked at him with suspicion. They distrusted anyone who did not share their anger, paranoia, and mindless destructiveness.

Zamora had reason to fear them. He was a simple boy from a small mountain town in Mexico who didn't even speak English. After a few days passed and the terror in his eyes subsided, I approached him. I decided to teach Zamora enough English to survive in jail. He grinned when he sensed that I was going to help him. I made flash cards of the alphabet out of toilet paper. He was an eager student and learned the entire alphabet in just two days. But he still didn't have any idea what the words he was learning meant.

A volunteer jail visitor brought me an English-Spanish dictionary that I gave to Zamora. With the help of me and the other men in the cell, Zamora soon learned English. He became our mascot and the little brother we all needed.

**A Special Christmas Gift.** Zamora asked me to help him
learn to read the Bible. I selected the Christmas story in
Luke. A week before Christmas, the volunteer church visitors were stunned and joyful as Zamora read the Christmas
story in nearly perfect English. Many eyes filled with
tears. My own eyes were damp. I was proud of Zamora. At
that time it seemed as though I was looking into the innocent face of a young Jesus.

With Christmas a few days away, I wondered what I
could give to Zamora to celebrate his new victory. My
lawyer brought me a large color picture of Jesus. It was
beautiful and even seemed to have Hispanic features. What
better way to cement our friendship and celebrate his learning English than to give him this picture? When I looked
at the peaceful, beautiful face, I realized what a contrast it
was to the fear, hurt, and loneliness we experience in jail.

Two days before Christmas, I surprised Zamora with the
picture of Jesus. Tears filled his eyes as he accepted this special Christmas gift. It was at that moment that I realized
that he had a family somewhere in Mexico wondering
where he was. His family must have taught him to love
Jesus. We hung the picture on the jail house wall, and all
the prisoners seemed pleased.

**Welcoming Jesus into Our Cell.** The day before Christmas,
the guards ordered all pictures taken down from the walls.
I asked if the picture of Jesus could be left up through
Christmas. The answer was "no," under the threat of additional punishment. Anger in our cell house rose in protest.
In spite of the threat of punishment, we all agreed to keep
the picture of Jesus on the wall. To our surprise, there was
no objection from the guards.

It is typical that, as Christmas Eve arrives, emotions in a jail will run high and tensions will mount as prisoners—deprived of normal social interaction with loved ones—strike out in anger and frustration at one another. Even though we still felt the tension, we also noticed a strange peace in our crowded cell. While fights broke out in other cells, there were none in ours.

Just before bedtime, I asked Zamora if he wanted to say the Lord's Prayer in his beautiful native Spanish. When he finished, I joined him in saying that beautiful healing prayer in English. There was no doubt that Christ was with us that night in jail.

On Christmas morning, the picture of Jesus still hung on our wall. Somehow now it didn't even matter if they were to order it removed. After all, wasn't Jesus in our hearts and actions? We all had a new appreciation of the power of love that Jesus represented to us. "Feliz Navidad," I wished Zamora in my clumsy Spanish.

"Merry Christmas, Lou," he replied in nearly perfect English. It seemed a strange place for me to find peace on earth at Christmas—in a jail cell. ■

# 16

# In His Hands

**by Maurice McDonald**

I had come through my annual physical examination with flying colors; everything seemed to be in fine working order, and life was good, praise God! My euphoria was to be short-lived, however. The next day my doctor phoned to say that my blood tests suggested something was amiss. "Come in and let us run the tests again, just to be sure there hasn't been a lab error." The second tests confirmed what the first had revealed: something inside of me had gone wrong. Further probing was strongly suggested, so we scheduled additional procedures.

When the exploratory processes were completed, my doctor arrived at my bedside just as I was coming out of the anesthetic. His solemn expression told me that he was not the bearer of happy tidings. "Well," he said, "I have some good news and some bad." I opted to hear the bad news first. "You have a cancer in your colon (large intestine) which needs to be removed immediately." This captured my attention so completely that I don't recall what constituted the good news.

**Total Peace.** Even as he showed me an ugly color photo-graph of the cancerous area, I had a sense of total peace. He might well have been talking about someone else for all the concern I was experiencing. My automatic response was to ask what steps we should take, and when. As I looked back on this moment later, I was somewhat sur-prised by the fact that I felt no fear or anxiety. Eventually I came to realize that this serenity was the product of twenty years of prayer, twenty years of spiritual growth since I first came to know and accept the Lord's love in a Christian community, and twenty years—indeed, a life-time—of intercession by others on my behalf.

I was admitted to the hospital that same afternoon and underwent surgery the following day. In the process of the operation, cancer was also found and removed from the wall of my abdominal cavity and lymph nodes. My oncol-ogist felt that surgery was not advisable—at least not at that time—for the cancer found in my liver.

Two days earlier, I had shot my best round of golf that year; now I was a cancer victim facing an uncertain future. When I asked my doctor's assistant for a prognosis, she said: "You're a stage four cancer victim. Less than five percent of cases like yours survive as long as two years." I was grateful for her candor. Later, I learned that the sur-geon who operated on me had told my family that I would surely die as a result of these cancers. It struck me how vulnerable people are and how little we are able to control the circumstances of our lives. Sometimes we have to be brought face to face with the reality of our inabili-ties before we will acknowledge that we truly are in God's hands. And what better place could we wish to be?

All of us probably have fantasized at one time or

another about how we would react to some sudden development that could bring us close to the precipice. Would we be brave? Would we panic? Would we put on a noble facade that would evoke wonder and praise from our family and friends? Would we totally lose it, dissolving into grief, hysteria, or depression? Perhaps we would grit our teeth and make courageous proclamations about our intention not to go down without a fight.

**The Prospect of Death.** During my service in World War II as an Air Corps tail gunner, the prospect of death was not unfamiliar, but I discovered that one can learn to live with it. The truth is that our responses are often just a reflection of where we stand in our relationship with the Lord. Logically, why should we be apprehensive about going to live forever in the presence of the God who loves us?

The prescribed course of treatment for my condition was a form of chemotherapy that is supposed to be relatively gentle to the system and had only a few mild side effects. It required my attendance at an infusion center once a week for six weeks, followed by a two-week layoff before beginning a new six-week cycle. During the layoff, CAT scans would be done to measure whatever progress—if any—was being made. This process would continue until my condition required something else.

The infusion center proved to be a happy surprise. I had been imagining a dreary, forlorn, clinical atmosphere where the doomed and the near-dead huddled in their cubicles, awaiting with hollowed eyes the inevitable coming of the Grim Reaper. In fact, the center had a distinctly upbeat environment, despite the obvious gravity of some patients' conditions. Many people spoke openly about their relationship with the Lord, about the peace they were experiencing through the grace of God, and of the consolation they were receiving through prayer. Jews and Christians, white and black, young and old alike, testified to the strength they were finding in God.

**The Sweetness of Life.** In the meantime, my awareness of the sweetness of life was being sharpened unbelievably. I felt joy in my life more keenly than I ever had before. Furthermore, I suspect that my golf partners were going out of their way to play badly so that my own golfing inadequacies would not be too discouraging to me. Greater love than this has no golfer!

Prayer took on a deeper meaning for me, not only my own prayer but the prayer of family, friends, and particularly the prayers of brothers and sisters in Christ. When the word went around about my diagnosis, the outpouring of encouragement, love, and support was awesome. Nor was there any lack of practical help. Neighbors, relatives, casual acquaintances, and close friends let us know that they would be there for us without fail, asking how and when they could help.

My wife, Ginny, has been and still is a rock of faith and love, and my four children have been a source of strength and assurance. As Ginny was praying for me one day, the Holy Spirit directed her to Psalm 91, the end of which reads as follows:

Because he cleaves to me in love, I will deliver him;
I will protect him, because he knows my name. When
he calls to me, I will answer him; I will be with him in
trouble, I will rescue him and honor him. With long
life I will satisfy him, and show him my salvation.

I have a number of Bibles. Some of them are such a hodgepodge of handwritten notes and underlinings that the text is barely legible. But I have one Bible which I do not mark; I keep it clean for use in prayer and study. When I went to look up Psalm 91 in this Bible, I found that it was the only verse in the entire Bible that had been underlined, even though neither of us has any recollection of having done so. One of God's little extras!

One of the things that surprised me was that some people did not seem comfortable about how they should react to my illness. It was not that they were lacking in love or concern for me and my family; quite the contrary. But there was a tendency to overreact, almost as though they were afraid to be seen openly enjoying life, lest I suffer from some gloomy reflection on my own allotted time. One suggestion I offer to friends and loved ones of those who are gravely ill: Be straightforward about their ailments and try to contribute to their joy, rather than share in their grief.

It is true that our days are numbered, but that is so from the moment we are conceived in our mother's womb. Our focus on the prospect of departing this world for a new and better life should not make us dreary, fill us with foreboding, or quench our joy. Quite the opposite; we should rejoice as we contemplate the happiness that awaits us. "No eye has seen, no ear has heard, no mind has conceived what God has prepared for those who love him" (1 Corinthians 2:9).

This whole experience began in the summer of 1996. Today I continue to receive chemotherapy on a weekly basis. No new cancers have been detected and the liver sites are at least being held in check. Physically, I feel as hearty as I have ever felt in my life, albeit a little creakier as I enter my seventy-second year.

As I write this testimony on a warm spring afternoon, the blossoming trees and shrubs around my home seem to be exuding a sweeter fragrance than I can ever remember; the simple joys of a brilliant sunset or a breezy day are delicious to all my senses; and the affection of my family and friends is more precious than ever. In short, life is increasingly lovely and more enjoyable. The reason is that God is closer and more real than ever before. And he is a God of love. ■

Maurice McDonald died of cancer on June 27, 1998.

# 17

# God Is Doing Time with Me

### by Kenneth G.

I'm just an ordinary man who had many problems. But now I'd like to tell you how those problems have been turned around.

I'd been involved in just about every kind of problem and sin that you can imagine in my forty-two years of living. Drug addiction, crime sprees, sexual immorality, total disregard for all types of authority—you name it, and I probably was involved in it. I lost my wife and two loving, beautiful children because of drugs. I lost good jobs and even good businesses. I'd gone from profession to profession, relationship to relationship, always looking for happiness to fill me up inside, but I never found it. Then, in 1996, I lost a really good job and turned again to drugs and crime.

**No Help in Sight.** One afternoon early in December 1997, I found myself surrounded by a group of FBI agents and sheriffs, with guns held to my head. I was being arrested for a federal crime. Desperate thoughts raced through my mind as I was handcuffed and strip-searched. I knew that there was a possibility that I would never get out of prison again. In those few moments, my life fell apart around me. I was totally lost, and could see no light at the end of the tunnel.

That night, as I stared out the window of a cold, one-man cell in the Cumberland County Jail in Portland, Maine, where I was awaiting extradition, I felt hopeless. There was no one to turn to, no one to help me. I'd heard a bit about Jesus Christ earlier in my life, but I couldn't imagine that he could do anything—or would want to—for such a wretched person as I was. I thought that I'd been too bad for God to love me. Little did I know then what a plan he had for me.

**Finding True Freedom.** Another inmate in the jail invited me to a Bible study the next evening. I went, and I heard the word of God really being proclaimed there. The message was strong and clear, and I started tossing it around in my mind. As I listened, I realized what a broken man I was. Then God's promise came alive to me: "He heals the brokenhearted and binds up their wounds" (Psalm 147:3). That night I turned to the Lord in faith and repentance and came to know his unconditional love for me.

Since that time, I feel as if a tremendous load has been lifted off me. I've found an inward peace and the real meaning of freedom, in spite of being confined in prison. God's love surrounds me. I can truly say with all my heart, "Blessed be the God and Father of our Lord Jesus Christ, the Father of mercies and God of all comfort" (2 Corinthians 1:3), because I've come to know his mercies and comfort myself.

**Doing Time with God.** I'm serving a ten-year prison sentence, but that doesn't matter much to me now. Knowing that I have a God who is loving, merciful, kind, and always there is what's become most important to me. God is doing time with me.

Every day I see God do new things with me, and I'm trying to let him have his way with me. One day as I was reading the Bible, I was really struck by the verses, "Do you not know that your body is a temple of the Holy Spirit within you, which you have from God? You are not your own; you were bought with a price. So glorify God in your body" (1 Corinthians 6:19-20).

God seemed to be speaking directly to me through those words. I'd been a smoker for twenty-two years—one pack or so a day. Suddenly I realized that I was dishonoring and abusing the body that God had given me, which is to be a dwelling place for his Holy Spirit. That's when I got rid of more of the baggage that I'd been carrying so long. I gave Jesus one hundred percent of me. I put the cigarette down, and now I'm smoke-free. Giving up cigarettes and smoking has actually been a joy to me, because I love Jesus so much and owe my life to him.

Since turning my life over to Jesus Christ, I've been set free from many of the sins and compulsions that were driving my life before. If God has given me such freedom inside a federal prison, imagine what he can do for you. He's just waiting for you to reach out to him like I did. ■

# 18

# Setting the Captives Free

### by Louis Grams

*Unrolling the scroll, Jesus found the place where it is written: "The Spirit of the Lord is on me, for he has anointed me to bring the good news to the afflicted. He has sent me to proclaim liberty to the captives, sight to the blind, to let the oppressed go free, to proclaim a year of favor from the Lord." . . . Then he began to speak to them, "This text is being fulfilled today even while you are listening."* (Luke 4:17-21)

Just as they were at that synagogue in Capernaum, these words continue to be fulfilled in our midst. Jesus our Savior continues to work among us in power. He manifests his love and power to increase our faith and draw us to him so that, united with him, we can give glory to our Father in heaven. I stand today as a witness to these glorious truths.

Thirty years ago, I started experiencing a variety of very strange medical problems, especially joint and respiratory problems. It got to the point that, every few months, there would be some major medical crisis. Three years ago, my doctor suggested that I see a rheumatologist. After many tests, he discovered that I had a rare immune system disorder that gradually destroys the small blood vessels and so inhibits circulation to the joints and major organs. The disease is incurable and typically fatal. I ended up having to quit work and virtually every other activity. I was on twenty different drugs, including chemotherapy, steroids, and insulin. It became difficult to think, and—what was even more frustrating—it became very difficult to pray.

Two years of being out of work gave me plenty of time to look at my life and my sins, failures, and weaknesses. I had a chance to repent of them and ask God to forgive me. Somehow I convinced myself that it would be better to die, because I saw that after thirty-five years of trying to live an adult Christian life, I was just as capable of sin as I was at the beginning. I continued to wrestle with an ego that too often saw itself as the center of the universe. There were times when I thought, "I don't want to go back to living that way. I want to be free. Wouldn't this be a good time to go?"

In the spring of 1997, after repeated trips to the emergency room, five hospitalizations, chronic pain, daily sickness, nausea, and fatigue, I was hospitalized with congestive heart failure and respiratory failure. Then I went into kidney failure as well. My doctor gently told my wife, Nancy, that he was afraid that they were just too late in addressing the underlying disease and that nothing could be done.

**Casting Out Fear.** The second day I was in the hospital, a nurse's aide whom I had not yet met walked into the room. She was a tall, rather large woman and had a good deal of authority just by her physical presence. She said,

"Have you got any fear?" I said, "Yes." I was at peace with death, but drowning in my own body fluids was not the way I wanted to die. She said, "Good. Jesus told me to come in here and tell you not to be afraid because he is here with you right now." I said, "I believe that." She pointed to my Bible and said, "You've got all the help you need right there." Then she paused and said, "He also told me to come in here and tell you that starting right now, this very moment, he's healing you. You need to be patient because it is going to take some time. But he is healing you. Be faithful to him because you know he will be faithful to you."

She left the room without saying another word. I was stunned and not sure what to think, but I was also at peace. (I've been asked many times since then if she was a member of the cast of *Touched by an Angel*.) About ten minutes later, a good friend of mine—a Catholic priest—walked in and asked if I wanted to be anointed and prayed over. As he was praying, I thought, "I don't have a reason for fear. The Lord is here and he will heal me. It might take him a long, long time"—I was thinking maybe fifteen or twenty years—"but he will heal me." For the next few days, however, things did not get better. In fact, they got worse before I started to gradually improve.

The day before I got out of the hospital, my lung doctor came in, very confused. He said, "I don't understand it. I've seen the damage to your lungs, but the lung scan we just did is the cleanest I've ever seen in my life. Your lungs are perfect." Two weeks later, my cardiologist—expecting the worst—was surprised to find my heart to be like new. But I was still not sure what God was up to. I still felt lousy most of the time, and my primary care doctor was still expecting another crisis.

**Out of the Desert.** One week later, at a retreat, some of my Christian brothers asked to pray with me because they believed God was healing me, and they wanted him to complete the healing. Before we prayed, we took time to repent of fears and doubts we all harbored. Then as we prayed, the desert inside of me that had made it so difficult to pray and even to think suddenly disappeared. It was as if a well had sprung open in my heart and I was drinking living water. I could think. I could talk. I could relate. I felt God's healing power. Pain and fear left me.

Within hours, persistent nausea, joint pains, and migraine headaches all ended. My racing heart settled down to a normal rate. My lung capacity increased to 150 percent of normal, and the chronic swelling in my legs went away. I went for a mile-and-a-half walk with my son. A week before that, I couldn't walk fifty feet. I started laughing all the time because it was so incredible to see what God was doing.

My doctors all agreed that there was no medical or psychological explanation for what happened. With tears in his eyes, my primary care doctor said, "What a great gift from God." He really thought he had lost me. But God has given me life and health and strength. He has set me free not only physically, but he has set my heart free from so many things that had been burdening me. Sins that I had wrestled with for years all of a sudden aren't a struggle. It's not that I never experience temptation, but there's a new strength, grace, and power to deal with it. I'm not interested in being the center of the universe. My life revolves around one Lord, and his name is Jesus.

**Setting Us Free.** I can remember seeing other people experience healing or some great transformation at the hands of the Lord and thinking to myself, "That's not fair. It's too easy. God couldn't possibly want to do it that way. Aren't we supposed to suffer and struggle to make our way to heaven?" There may be a lot of suffering and struggling in our lives, but that is not what makes our way into heaven. Only Jesus makes that way for us. Only Jesus brings us into real freedom. He allows us to share in his suffering, struggle, and pain and to find cause for rejoicing in it all, because we know we will share in his resurrection.

Since my own healing, I've seen the Lord at work again and again in many people's lives. I've seen countless healings and wondrous signs of his power and love.

Jesus is here for us. He is here in power. He wants to set us free and to make us one with him so that we all can say: "The Spirit of the Lord is on me, for he has anointed me to bring the good news to the afflicted. He has sent me to proclaim liberty to the captives, sight to the blind, to let the oppressed go free, to proclaim a year of favor from the Lord." ■

# 19

# With the Lord in the Land of the Living

**by Mary Rita P.**

I came home from my job as an ophthalmic technician one evening in February 1992, feeling drained. I had just assisted in a new type of lens implant surgery, and my head ached. David, my husband, tried to talk to me, but I felt confused. The next thing I remember, I was being carried out of the front door of my home on a stretcher.

The doctors at our local hospital told me I had experienced a grand mal seizure. They ordered tests and found that I had a mass in my brain—some kind of a tumor. When my doctor gave me his diagnosis, I thought I was dreaming.

Surgery was quickly scheduled. The night before I went into the hospital, I visited my parish priest for the sacrament of the anointing of the sick. He reminded me that I would need to accept God's will in my life, whatever that might be. I felt there was no way that God would want me to have cancer. After all, I was the parish organist, a choir member and church cantor. The truth was that I still wanted to be in charge of my life, and I reminded God of all the things I had been doing for him.

**A New Path.** It didn't take long to get a preliminary pathology report. When the doctor said the word "malignant," my heart sank; I felt very low. I had been so certain that God wanted me to continue my charmed life so that I could keep working for him. I never gave a thought to the fact that God might want me to take a new path. After several additional tests, we learned that the tumor was an aggressive type. My surgeon recommended—rather tactlessly, I thought—that David and I not postpone any travel plans, in case I failed to live out the year.

I began a course of radiation, which required me to leave for work an hour early each day—a tiring ordeal. As my hair began to fall out, I went to my office each day wearing a color-coordinated beret. When my vision became blurry one day, I was referred to another neurosurgeon who recommended an operation to remove the tumor. Again I was admitted into the hospital.

Wearing a metal "halo"—a necessary preoperative procedure—I sat up for a while the night before my surgery to read my Bible. Every time I opened the Scriptures, the Lord led me to passages that offered encouragement. One psalm especially spoke to me: "You have delivered my soul from death, my eyes from tears, my feet from stumbling; I walk before the LORD in the land of the living" (Psalm 116:8-9). Jesus seemed to be talking to me directly, telling me not to worry.

The chemotherapy I received after the surgery was a new type that could be toxic to lung tissue. My physician ordered a lung function test, and it was discovered that my lung capacity had been cut to sixty percent efficiency. I hadn't been doing any church singing, but when I tried, I was sharply aware of my loss. I was switched to a new chemo drug, which made my hair fall out all over again. No voice, no hair! The Lord was making me totally dependent on him.

**A Leap of Faith.** During all of these ups and downs, I prayed every day. It seems that whenever I felt the lowest, the Lord directed me to the precise Scripture passage that was meant for me. This gave me hope. I also began to pray with my husband David every day. As a result, he decided to become a Catholic, and I was privileged to be his confirmation sponsor. We both experienced a leap of faith, knowing that we were never alone with the Lord at our side and in our hearts.

A month after my diagnosis, a group of dedicated friends started coming to my home every week to pray the rosary with me and to pray for my health. There were times when I was too sick to join the group. At those times my mother was always there to stand in my place, which was like being there in spirit.

My progress was slow, but real. I had an obvious left-sided weakness, and a facial droop that caused me to slur words, drool, and have a crooked smile. I needed to walk with a four-pronged cane. Yet I knew that since I was still alive, the Lord had something in mind for me. He began to show me that he would direct me in my new life if I turned it over to him. The group of friends that had gathered to pray for me continued to meet at my house on Tuesday nights, and they still do today—four and a half years later. Sometimes as many as fifteen people come— even in bad weather—and we have a prayer meeting and pray the rosary. One of the members of the group became very ill and lapsed into a coma. We prayed for him, and he recovered.

I am unable to keep up with the busy pace at the ophthalmology practice but, since I no longer have a full-time job, I have more time to visit sick friends, attend a Bible study, and do volunteer work. I can no longer play the organ or sing at my church as I had done for years, but the Lord blessed that situation too. When I was in the choir loft, my husband didn't feel comfortable going to church alone. He was not Catholic, and there was nobody to sit with him. Now he has become Catholic, and we sit together during Mass. He is very active in the parish; he's even on the parish council.

**A Witness to God's Mercy.** Although God had extended my life, I found out that he wanted to do still more. In 1994, I attended an out-of-town healing service. With Mary acting as intercessor, the Lord healed my facial droop. I left the service with a restored face, a renewed faith, and a never-ending smile.

My left arm and leg, however, were still very weak. A year later, in 1995, I attended another healing service. The priest poured oil over the right side of my head, where the tumor had been. Gradually, with more therapy, my left leg has grown stronger, to the point where I can drive my car and walk a whole mile, using only a single cane.

My life has certainly changed. What I thought to be so important—that I do God's work—turned out to be not as important to God. I am certain that he led me through this difficult experience to be a witness to his healing power and love. When I cried out to him, he heard me and comforted me. In his mercy, he allowed me to keep on living. I thank him for each day of life he gives me—many more than were predicted. He alone is the Divine Healer, healing us not just physically, but emotionally and spiritually as well. ■

# 20

# I Know Someone Is Listening

### by William Hilditch

I was raised as a good Catholic and even made my First Holy Communion. But then, when I was in the first grade, my parents got divorced, and my three brothers and I were put into a foster home. Later, my older brother and I were sent to one orphanage, and my two younger brothers were sent to another. From there, I was shifted to six different foster homes. Once I got to feel at home with one of the families, they would move me to another. I guess that's why they tell you not to get too attached to any one family.

When I was about sixteen years old, my father got remarried and had my older brother and me move back with him. But my stepmother thought we were in the way, so she made it hard for me to stay around. In the end, I ran away. That's when I started getting into trouble because I was living on the streets. I had nowhere to live, nothing to eat, and no way to make money because I was too young to work. So I ended up in a training school for boys.

I got married young, and my first wife died having a baby. The baby died too. That's when I started drinking a lot and smoking marijuana. I wanted to cover up my sadness and loneliness. I just wanted to fit in some-where in life. I've been drinking ever since. I'm now forty-seven years old, and with the help of God and Alcoholics Anonymous, I pray I will never go back to that kind of life. And with the Holy Spirit guiding me this far, I'm beginning to feel better about myself.

I got into trouble with the law when my drinking and drug use took control of my life. I would be drink-ing, and the next day not remember what I did the day before. After ten years of marriage to my second wife, I found out she was going out with another man. I was drunk when I found out, and I don't know what hap-pened the rest of that night. The next day I woke up in jail, and my wife was in the hospital with a broken jaw. I guess I got scared that I would lose her and my family, and so I totally lost control.

**Talking to Jesus.** I experienced God's presence here in prison when I found that I had no one who cared about me or thought of me once I was locked up. Since coming here two years ago, I have received no mail. None of my so-called friends on the street have come to visit me. It's only now, after two years, that my older brother has started writing to me. So, for two years I would lay in my bunk and talk to Jesus and it really felt as if he was listening to me. God com-forted me by letting me know that there was someone who was listening and who stood by me through thick and thin.

God is more real to me now than when I thought that life was all about having material things. Now I have nothing at all, but I know what happiness really is.

My friendship with Jesus has grown a lot over the last two years. I've had time to talk with God and ask his forgiveness for all I've done wrong against him, my family, friends, and coworkers. I now feel more at ease with myself. God seems to take care of my every need just in time. Finally, I can go to sleep at night not worrying whether I will wake up alive the next morning. He's done so much, and as long as I do right and follow his commandments, I know he will take care of me.

**Losing Everything.** The hardest thing about being in prison is knowing I'm losing everything I wanted and worked for. My family turned against me, but now they are coming back because they see how much I am trying to change my life. They can see that I really want to make it out of here alive.

Sometimes I still wonder if I'm going to live from one day to the next. I worry whether someone will rob me while I'm in school or at my AA meeting. In prison, you always have to keep looking over your shoulder.

I would like for you to pray that I may get out soon and be a better Christian. I want to be able to give back to the community and just be a better all-around person. ■

# 21

# Through Christ Who
# Strengthens Me

**by Barbara Lavalley**

When my first daughter, Cassandra, was stillborn in 1986, some people asked me, "How can you believe in God?" My answer was, "How can I not?" I reached deep into my heart and remembered the times he had not let me down. I remembered the times he had remained by my side when I was more interested in my own will than his. Too many times, I had seen God's hand and felt his presence in my life. I could say, without a doubt, that God was there. However, since the loss of my seven-year-old daughter, I have found that he is with me more than I ever imagined possible.

Rachel died very unexpectedly on January 13, 1996. She went to bed with a little cold, but an acute and lethal viral infection closed off all her air passages. I have never known, and hope to never know again, such despair as I experienced at the loss of Rachel. I was sure it was not something I could live through. I knew I couldn't. But "through Christ who strengthens me" (Philippians 4:13), I am still here. Each morning when I wake up and realize all over again the reality of her not being here, I can only turn to God. I cannot do it alone. When the hole in my heart gapes

ever wider, he fills it with his grace. When I am not functioning and ready to give up, and my heart feels dead in my
chest, the Lord fills me with the love of the Holy Spirit, and
with the love of my family and friends.

**A Special Moment.** Even on the night Rachel died, I could
see God at work. He worked through the small voice of my
five-year-old son. While we were getting ready for bed that
night, he asked unexpectedly, "What would you do if one
of us died?" I was speechless. He said, "Never mind." But
I could not let it go. For some reason, he had said it, and
so we talked about it. As I put Rachel to bed, the subject
was still on my mind. Rachel and I talked about dying, and
how we would always be together, no matter where we
were. We talked about our love for one another and the
special things we liked about one another. Without knowing it, we were saying good-bye. I will never forget the
things we said to each other that night. Our last words
were, "I love you." I stayed beside her, and she fell asleep
with her head on my heart. I remember thinking, "Lord,
never let me forget this moment."

How could I be angry with a God who allowed me such
a moment and such memories? I could have rushed her to
bed, busy with other things. But that evening was special—
I knew it even before she died later that night.

I don't know what my life would have been like this past
year if I had chosen to turn away from God. I could have
chosen bitterness and despair, but I've realized that it is a
choice. When I wake up each day, I can choose to lie face
down on the floor and refuse to start the day, but I have
learned that if I fall to my knees first and pray, I gain the
strength for one more day. If during the day I feel like

repeatedly banging my head against a wall, I pray. I know that in the beginning, when I could not even pray, that people were praying for me. God was here for me even then. I have not felt, for even one day, that God was not comforting me in some way.

**God Cares About Our Needs.** In my grief, Rachel came to me one evening, holding someone's hand, and said, "Mama, I'm with God." I knew in that moment that God cares about even the least of us. He cares about our individual needs. My need was to know where my daughter was, and that she was not afraid. I knew that when she died in my arms, she awoke in God's. I did not see God, but he allowed me to see Rachel. This gave me the hope I needed to survive, and to be a useful person on this earth until the time when we will be together again—not only with Rachel and Cassandra, but with a God who cares so much for us.

God has taken a very active part in our lives. After Rachel died, I was concerned about the reactions of the children in her second-grade class. I was inspired to take Rachel's stuffed animals and give them to each child directly after the funeral. I asked them to please love them for Rachel so they would have something to hold onto that would comfort them.

When we were struggling to decide whether to stay in our home after Rachel's death, I took it to God in prayer. We could not make a decision—it was too heart-wrenching to move. I said, "Lord, if it is your will that we move, please let our house sell within a month, or not at all." I heard him say, "I don't need even a week." Our house sold the first day it was on the market.

**A Love Stronger Than Death.** When I've wanted my way—to have Rachel back—God is still there, and I feel that he cries with me. His love is big enough to stretch around all of my hurt. When my younger son comes to me with his aching heart, God stretches his arms wider, and even wider still for my nineteen-year-old and my husband. We have found his love to be bigger—and stronger—than death.

My life will never be the same. Even though I know it will always be a struggle, my hope is in a God who never changes, a God who is there for us in the good times and the bad. If I believe in God's love in the good times, how can I not believe in his love during the difficulties? I may not understand why, but every day he gives me courage when I am afraid, and comfort when I am in despair. He helps me to continue to be a useful person, and my faith in a caring God is renewed.

That he could have chosen to change the outcome doesn't matter to me anymore; that he has not left me during this time is where I have found my faith. If we let him, he will carry our pain. If we let him, he will strengthen us in all things. ■

# 22

# My Calvary, My Cross

**by William J. Zalot**

This morning begins like many others, as I pull myself from my bed to my wheelchair at 6:30 and pray "The Morning Offering." I grab my battery-operated recharge-able shaver. By 6:45, I am ready to spend the next fifteen minutes with Our Lady as I recite the rosary. Today, being Monday, I meditate on the joyful mysteries.

As I get to the fourth joyful mystery, I recall Simeon's words to Mary: "A sword will pierce your own soul, so the secret thoughts of many may be revealed" (Luke 2:35). I've shared many of my sorrows as well as my joys with her, and I recall some of them as I pray. It is 6:55 as I conclude the "Glory Be" and "O My Jesus." I must call Dad at 7:00, for my ride will arrive for Mass at 8:00.

**A Heavy Burden.** I watch my father draw my bath water. Today, the burden of this feels especially heavy. Yet in his actions, I feel the warmth of our heavenly Father's love. Part of every single day's mountain, or cross, is to swallow my pride and allow a man thirty years my senior to bathe and dress me, a routine he has repeated all my life. Dad backs me into the tub and bathes me, as he has done since I was a small child. By this time I realize this is another splinter in the cross that God has given me. Yet, facing this cross helps me to climb the steeper mountains of the day. Before I leave home, Dad dresses me, as he would dress a grandson—though I'm a man of forty-one.

This part of the mountain climb ends at 7:30, and now I take time to reflect on the Mass readings using *The Word Among Us*, as I've done for over a decade. I read the passages and accompanying meditation. I then put on my coat; it is 7:55. My ride arrives at 8:00 exactly.

We reach the church at 8:15 and I slip into my wheelchair. I hope I have a chance to see the priest before Mass, for I want him to hear my confession. He agrees, and I am thankful. Within moments, Mass begins, and I can receive the Eucharist with a clear conscience.

This portion of the day is my high point, and it makes the rest of the day less burdensome, as I am reminded that I am offering up the humiliation of my dependency for those who have left the church as well as for those souls who are in purgatory. It's during these sixteen hours of the day, after all, that I have the privilege of sharing my faith with CCD students and speaking with different groups about issues related to disability. Then there is the constant privilege of giving glory to God through my limitations, not focusing only on my special needs.

The days are relatively easy, but the nights are lonely and long. Being single, a deep sense of loneliness and the vulnerability of my dependency on my father at his age comes over me. This is when I must trust in my heavenly Father, praying, "Father, into your hands I commit my spirit!" (Luke 23:46). May I say with an affirming voice, "Your will, not mine, be done" (22:42). Both my earthly father and my heavenly Father watch over me. These two fathers protect me. ■

# 23

# Discovering a God Who Cares

### by Richard Parker

I was born into a large, proud family in Corpus Christi, Texas. My mother is Catholic, and my brothers and sisters and I attended Mass every Sunday along with catechism classes. We all did this until we were old enough to leave home.

I wanted to be rich, successful, ruthless, and proud. I also wanted to do my own thing and have all the fun and pleasure I could get out of life. All my older brothers and sisters are successful, and I was going to try and top them all. The problem was that I did not succeed at this.

As a teenager, I got busted several times for minor offenses and for dangerous drugs and paraphernalia. In my twenties, I joined the infantry for four years, picked up two years of college, and got married. In my thirties, I tried to become successful but never made enough money and argued constantly with my wife. We were basically atheistic, alcoholic, and unhappy with our love life. We did have three beautiful children whom we love very much. In my forties, I got divorced, lost my job, my savings, my house, my arrogant pride, and my freedom.

Today I am forty-seven years old and have been locked up for six years. I have a forty-five-year sentence for burglary with intent to commit aggravated assault and injury to an elderly man.

**Other Gods.** My gods were women, money, and beer. I was bankrupt, so I injected myself with the last one hundred dollars' worth of cocaine I could afford. From this, I went berserk and can hardly remember anything. I only remember crashing into two homes, punching one man in the face once and hitting another man on the arm with a hammer. Fortunately, no one got seriously injured that night, except for me and my reputation, my worldly pride, and any chance of earthly success.

God has tried to get my attention many times throughout my life. The first time, I was in the army. I was lonely, and God answered one of my prayers. I rejoiced to know that there was a God and went to church a few times. After awhile, though, my love of beer and my lust for women pulled me away from my faith.

The second time, I was out of jail on bond and attending Alcoholics Anonymous meetings. After getting a sponsor and working the twelve-step program, I felt that I had a spiritual awakening. I lost that spiritual feeling when I got involved with a woman who was also attending the AA meetings. When we broke up, I went back to drinking and doubting.

The third time I came to believe in God, I was in jail waiting to go to court. I was afraid of a long prison sentence. A Baptist friend of mine gave me a prayer to say and I said it, and again I felt like I had a spiritual awakening. From this experience, I was able to become smoke-free, and that had seemed impossible for me. With all of God's love, I still received a forty-five-year sentence. Despair overcame me and again I fell into doubt.

I was angry with God because he just didn't make sense. It is important for me to understand what I believe. I reasoned that if I can't understand, I wasn't even going to think about God or worry about him. If he is all loving, like they say, he would understand. With all this finding and losing faith or favor with God, I felt a little like the Israel of the Old Testament.

**Finding God Again.** Finally, I have found God again. I certainly hope and pray that I can persevere until the end of my earthly days. For the past two and one-half years, God has been very active in my life. It began when I found out that my daughter Cindy had cancer. She had less than a fifty percent chance for survival. The tumor was the size of a golf ball and had spread to her lymph nodes.

It took me about a week of misery to finally get on my knees and ask God for his help. An acquaintance of mine suggested that I go to a healing prayer service. I don't know if it was this prayer service or my pitiful offer of devotion to God, but my daughter's tumor simply disappeared. I was amazed, to say the least, and I started going to every church and church program that I could attend.

It can get very confusing going to different religious groups and hearing all the different theologies of what you have to do to be saved. I felt, and know from experience, that if I didn't come out of my confusion soon, my faith would suffer.

So I did the same thing again that I did when my daughter was sick. I got on my knees, and asked God to give me the answer. I asked the Lord, "Which denomination should I belong to?" Immediately after saying this prayer, I decided to study my Spanish conversation book. I opened the book and there was a newspaper picture of my daughter Cindy. It was taken before anyone knew she had cancer. It showed her playing tennis for her high school team. I don't know how this picture got into my Spanish book. It was supposed to be with my photo album. On the same page with my daughter's picture was a picture of two Catholic priests with a Catholic church in the background. This, I feel, was my answer.

God seemed to quickly make available to me the Catechism of the Catholic Church. I began attending Mass and staying for RCIA. Even though I had spent my adolescent years going to one hour of catechism every week, I now found out how little I knew about my church. What I have now learned has really helped me to understand and accept God. It all makes so much sense.

Today I am happy to have a personal relationship with God. I believe in the love and patience he offers everyone. He is a good God who forgives all who are sincere. When I can be completely obedient to him, he draws very close to my heart. When I fail to be obedient, he is quick and friendly to forgive me through the sacrament of reconciliation. He answers many of my prayers. He answers my prayers in awesome ways. I keep a daily journal of all the blessings he has given me. I can never again say that there is no God or that he doesn't care. ■

# 24

# Through Him All Things Are Possible

### by Lucille MacPherson

I began my teaching career in a junior high school when I was twenty-two years old. By the time I was twenty-six, I had worked my way up to the head of the language department at a nearby senior high school and was already being groomed for administration. I was married at the time, and my husband and I owned a sporting goods store with a partner. Through our contacts in the store, we became friends with some high-profile National Hockey League players, and our social calendar was very full. Life was good, and we were on our way to (worldly) success.

**Crying Out for Help.** A few years later, in 1987, my world came crashing down around me. My husband didn't seem to know I existed. He used so many drugs that he became oblivious to my attempts to sit down with him and work things out. My marriage was failing, and the business began to fail as well. I was crying out for help, and what resulted was a criminal record for a fraudulent purchase and the humiliation of going to court, posing for a mug shot, and being fingerprinted. This was the lowest time in my life. I wanted to curl up and die. It was at this point, when I knew I could not repair things on my own, that the Lord showed himself to me.

Some months after separating from my husband, I met a wonderful Christian man. He attended Mass on Sundays and invited me to come along. Being Catholic myself, I decided it was about time I returned to the church. Soon after, this man's mother (my future mother-in-law) invited the two of us to a Get to Know Jesus overnight retreat. It was Palm Sunday of 1989, and during the course of that retreat, I experienced a love that I had never felt before.

That weekend, I accepted the Lord into my life and began an incredible transformation that has touched every part of my life. My compulsion to work my way to the top didn't seem important to me anymore. Because of the company I had kept in the past, I had a strong desire to keep up with the Joneses. The accumulation of material possessions was important to me; I considered it a sign of success. But the Lord replaced that drive with a desire to seek him, to know him, and to love him. I began to seek Christian friends and attended as many Christian conferences and seminars as possible.

But the Lord did not rest at that. He had much more in store for me. He wanted to heal me of the horrors I had endured as a child. He wanted me to be whole so that I could be the person he created me to be.

**Healing Wounds from the Past.** In the fall of 1991, my life took another turn. I was forced to take a leave from my teaching position due to stress and begin a healing process that would last many months. For years, I had denied the severity of the pain I carried since I was a little girl. "Severe sexual abuse" were the words that were impressed upon my memory as I left my therapist's office. I had experienced abuse at the hands of my great-grandfather from as early as I could remember, and then at the hands of my own father between the ages of five and fourteen. I was further assaulted at fourteen by a friend of the family.

Because of this trauma, I had become an extremely angry and fearful person. The greater part of my anger was directed toward my father for what he had done. He was supposed to be my protector, not my assailant. My fear of him never left me, even as an adult. I hated for him to touch me, and I cringed when he kissed me good-bye. If we were ever together in the same car, I clung desperately to the door waiting anxiously to arrive at our destination. I had spent so much of my energy being angry and fearful that it was finally getting the best of me.

The therapist I was seeing was very helpful, and we were making progress. Still, something seemed to be missing because the Christian dimension was not present. I decided that I had to let the Lord be a part of my healing process. I sought out a Christian counselor in Spokane, Washington.

**Reconciliation with My Father.** It was there, through prayer-filled counseling sessions, that the Lord healed me and took away my anger and fear. Over the course of a week in October of 1992, he replaced my anger and fear with a new-found love for my father that I never thought possible. For the first time in my life, I saw my father through the Lord's eyes. I suddenly had a desire to share with him how powerfully God's grace and mercy had changed me. I decided to go to his home to tell him personally that I forgave him and that I loved him. He wept, I wept, and the Lord bound us together as father and daughter once again.

Today, my father and I have a very loving relationship. I pray often that he too will turn to the Lord and find deeper peace and healing. How the Lord has transformed my life and restored my relationship with my father are beyond all human understanding. His grace and mercy are endless. Through him all things are possible. ■

# 25

# A Future and a Hope

### by Michael Thompson

*I know the plans I have for you, says the LORD, plans for*
*welfare and not for evil, to give you a future and a hope.*
(Jeremiah 29:11)

Today, that's one of my favorite verses in the Bible, but it didn't always reflect my life. I spent more than fifteen years in and out of prison, without any hope and without any plans or goals for my future. That all changed a few years ago when I came face to face with God's love.

**On My Street Corner.** Growing up in the inner city, I never heard the word "love" mentioned in my family—it was just a word for wimps. Both my parents died before I was fourteen, and good role models were few and far between. Even though I graduated from a Catholic high school, I didn't really know who God was.

Since I hadn't gotten much love during my teen years, I reached out for any attention I could get. I passed by an opportunity to go to college because I was living day by day, with no purpose or plans for the future. I wanted to be like the guy out on the corner with a big wad of money in his pocket and a nice car, getting his attention however he could, even if it was negative. So I began selling drugs, and wound up in prison for the first time when I was twenty-one years old.

That was the beginning of a vicious cycle for me that lasted seventeen years. I'd get out of prison and go back into my old environment and end right back in prison again. In between prison stints, I spent a lot of time just standing on the same street corner in town, a man without hope. One day as I was wasting my life there on my corner, the father of a friend of mine saw me and told me his son had gone to a ministry to street people and the homeless. When he said he could see some definite, positive changes in his son, I decided to go to the mission too.

**Overcome by Love.** When I walked through the rescue mission door on August 7, 1995, I was greeted with compassion and a hug. Slowly I began to experience God's love through those who cared for me at the mission. Over the next six months, the love that had been missing from my life became real to me, and the truths of the gospel began to sink into my mind and take hold of my heart. Finally, after so many years of living on my own strength and making a mess of my life, I surrendered to God.

The past four years since my conversion have been the best of my life. What I didn't have before, I have today: A future and a hope. I know who I am in Christ Jesus. I know why I was created. I know what my purpose is. There is a plan for my life. I have goals and good order in my life. I have a wife and a family and a home, and we live in a way that I believe is pleasing to God. Sure, I have troubles like everyone else, but I have something available to me now that I never had before—the Holy Spirit dwelling in me, giving me the strength to overcome difficulties and temptations and anything else that rises against me.

Now, when I look back on my life, I realize that my time in prison did something for me that I couldn't have done for myself: It pulled me out of an environment that was destroying me. I was killing myself out there on that street corner. We all take different journeys to get to the place where God can reach us. Sometimes we have to be beaten up and broken in order for God to come in and fix us. I was a broken man all those years. I had a big hole in my heart, and I tried to fill it with girls, with cars, with money, with drugs—but nothing ever sufficed or satisfied me. Now I thank God for even that rugged road in prison because it brought me to the place where I am today. I wouldn't change that for anything in the world.

**Living My New Life.** My life has become very stable since my conversion. I've grown in perseverance, and I'm learning what it means to have endurance. I've been able to tell my family and friends who had been harmed by my behavior how sorry I am for that. They are extremely happy with me and with what Jesus has done in my life. Since coming to know how much God loves me and how much he has forgiven me, I've also learned to forgive others. I've realized that holding on to things that were done to me unfairly just kept me in bondage, so now I've let go of all that.

Prayer has become important to me, too, because it's my communication with God and Jesus. When I'm not praying regularly, I miss out on much of what Jesus has made available for me. It's often in the time I spend in prayer with him that he reveals things to me. I also intercede for others so that they will come to know the love of God, that

they will be restored, that they will be healed for whatever
is needed in their lives.

**Hope in Jesus Christ.** Jesus comes to the needy and the
brokenhearted. There are many men and women in prison
who wound up there because there was no love in their
lives. If we reach out to these people and love them, their
lives can be changed. I can't think of anything else I'd
rather be doing now than working on staff at the rescue
mission. There are currently twelve men—all of whom
were in prison at one time or another—residing at the mission who came because of what God did in my life.

There is hope for the men and women who are incar-
cerated in prisons throughout the country. Hope that
comes from Jesus. Hope that doesn't cost anything. Hope
that is real and genuine. Hope that is available to anyone
who turns to Christ.

Jesus didn't come to save the righteous—he came to save
sinners. Those in prisons are often strong and full of
pride, and these are good qualities. But they also have to
become humble enough to accept when they are defeated.
Anyone who has spent time in prison, whether for one year
or ten, has been defeated. I know, because I was there. But
anyone who believes that Jesus is who he said he is and
humbly turns to him can receive the strength to live a new
life pleasing to God. I know, because I'm living that new
life now. Just as he promised, God has given me a future
and a hope. ■

# 26

# Prepare Us, O Lord!

### by Barbara Hughes

"God never gives us more than we can handle." I had heard that expression many times before, but it wasn't until after my family went through some major shake-ups that I knew for a fact that it was true. If we let him, the Lord helps us to handle any situation that we face. He will prepare us if we hand everything over to him. Of course, this is easier said than done. It takes practice and patience, since we always want to be in charge of our destinies and control our future. To give God the keys and let him drive takes so much faith and trust.

**A Devastating Illness.** It is devastating to have your child come down with an illness that a bandage, a hug, and kiss cannot cure. It's even worse when there is no cure at all for his sickness. In 1990, our son John was diagnosed with AIDS. The news was traumatic for me. I prayed and prayed. I even tried to make a deal with God: "Please, just fix John. He's only twenty-seven years old! I'll be good for the rest of my life—just don't let this happen to us. Please, make this thing go away and I'll do anything you say!" But it didn't go away. It stayed for almost three years, and we had to learn to live with it as it took over his life and ours.

Accepting this illness was difficult for John. At the time, AIDS was associated with homosexuals, and John was not gay. He was no saint, but he was very loving and kind and would do anything for his family and friends. John was in denial, and for a long time he blamed himself and didn't want people to know about it. He suffered a great deal, not only with physical pain, but with the pain that comes from knowing you have no future.

After a while, John had to move back home with us because he was not able to work at a full-time job and couldn't pay the rent. He got a little better and worked every now and then. He had a good attitude some of the time, but he could also get depressed and would try to escape with alcohol and drugs. It didn't help, of course; the disease was still there the next day when he woke up feeling badly. He spent many days in the hospital off and on through the years and really hated it, so we were not surprised when he said he didn't want to die in a hospital, but at home instead.

**Helping Our Son Meet Jesus.** We began to make preparations to take care of John at home. Our other children gathered around to help and support us, each one taking their turn to sit with John and to pray, read, and talk to him. Our priest came to give him the last rites and to pray with us. As I look back over the events of that last week of John's life, I can see God's hand in every detail. John received a gift not everyone receives. He was given a chance to say good-bye to his family and his friends.

John's death brought us all closer to God. We felt the Lord's presence throughout the week. His Spirit filled us with love and compassion as we worked side by side with one goal in mind—to help our John meet Jesus. I believe God prepared us for the challenge we had to face. If anyone had told me we could do what we did before the time came, I would have doubted it. John took his last breath on October 8, 1992, at about 10:30 p.m., after sitting up with eyes wide open and a big smile that only his father was privileged to see.

John always had a strong but quiet faith. He didn't talk much about it, but after he died we found many, many notebooks filled with poetry he had written. It was obvious our John had a much deeper faith than we ever imagined. I found this poem in his notebook next to his bed, dated February 6, 1992, eight months before he died:

Life and Love,
Alone and scared.
Life after death. Who knew?
Precious is life and endearing is love.
Death one way out. But who knew?
Keep the faith.
Let Jesus take your soul.
For he will deliver to the Lord
and upon his ship
We will all climb aboard.
Signed, John loves God. ( John Patrick Hughes)

**Drawing Strength from the Lord.** God's work is not finished in us yet. Recently, my husband was diagnosed as having Lou Gehrig's disease. It took us some time and much prayer to learn to deal with his disease. He now uses canes, a walker, and for some occasions a wheelchair; but his faith is strong and his spirits are high. There is no cure, so we have to learn to carry this cross. We go to daily Mass and say the rosary and divine chaplet. He is an example to the community of how faith can sustain you during trials and difficulties.

Through all these circumstances, I have learned to draw my sustenance from the Lord. At five o'clock each morning, I get up to pray, read the daily Scripture and other spiritual books, and write in my prayer journal. As the Lord builds my faith and trust, I feel an inner peace. He will give me the strength I need to see me through each day. ■

# 27

# The Time Is Now

**by Don H.**

When I was in prison, I worried about what I was going to do once I got out. I thought, "Where am I going to go? What's going to be out there for me once I'm released?" I knew what had happened each time I had gotten out of jail before—I had slipped right back into my old life and wound up in prison again.

It's lonely in prison, and there's plenty of time to think. I used to reflect on my past and what I'd done, and try to figure out the reasons why. Then I'd think, "What more does life have to offer than this? How is this all going to change? How can I change?" But nothing had ever changed. That is, not until God said, "The time is now."

**Doing Drugs and More.** During my early childhood there was a lot of love in my house. But when I was ten years old, Mom and Dad got divorced and our family life was torn apart. During the next several years I lived with my mother and stepfather, but I often visited my dad. When I was fifteen, I went to live with Dad—and that's when I started using marijuana.

My dad and stepmother were average, middle-class folks. But in the evenings, Dad would sit back and watch television and smoke a joint. I was curious and wondered what he was doing—and why I couldn't do the same—so I started asking questions. Dad told me that drugs would only lead to trouble, but then he handed me a joint and smoked it with me.

That was just the beginning of the trouble I got into. I was addicted to heroin for years. I did whatever it took to get it. A couple of times, I almost died of overdoses. But drug addiction wasn't my only problem. I was also charged once for armed robbery and once for kidnapping. I was in and out of county jails and detention centers.

**Trapped in the Cycle.** Every time I went to jail, I'd come clean. I didn't use drugs in jail, even though if you are looking for them, you can find them there. Looking back, I believe I was so worn out from my runs on the street that, once I got back into prison, I needed a break. I wanted to clean myself up. I didn't want to do drugs anymore, but I didn't know the way out.

Occasionally I read the Bible, especially when I felt lonely. Sometimes I went to the prison chaplain's services. I knew in my heart—I don't think it was in my head yet—that there was a better way to live. Still, each time I got out, I just fell back into my old way of life.

Then I went to prison in 1993 on a three-year sentence for child support issues and violation of probation. That's when I began to pray, "God, lead me to someone who can speak to me about my life."

When I was released in 1996, I began to do drugs again. The next year, a friend told me about Jesus, gave me a place to stay, and tried to help me clean up. I ended up back in jail for a few weeks, but got out on bail. By the second day out, I had started to use drugs again, but that's when I finally asked myself, "Do you believe what you heard about Jesus?" God's time had come. I seemed to hear him say, "The time is now."

**Encountering God's Love.** I knew I had to get myself to a place where there were other Christians, and so I went to a ministry for street people that I had heard about. Otherwise, I would have just continued to do what I'd been doing all along, and it would have only gotten worse. I'd finally been broken—and that's when I began to be honest with God and surrender to him.

I went to the ministry looking for Jesus—and I found him. I entered the house called "detox," where guys coming in off the streets come down from drugs or alcohol. I knew I was killing myself, and that everyone else around me was suffering from my actions too. I knew I didn't want to continue to live the way I had been. As I lay in bed in detox, I just said this prayer: "God, please forgive me. Come into my heart and show me the way."

I felt God's presence and his cleansing—and I heard a still, small voice say, "You are forgiven. You are forgiven no matter what you have done. You don't have to do it again. I will be faithful to you if you will be faithful to me."

God's love and mercy had brought me to this point. Now all I wanted was to listen and learn. Through the love and support of the people who cared for me and through the structure and discipline of the program there, my life began to change. I found Jesus as I read the Bible every day. I found him in prayer. I found him in others who had gone through the same struggles I had been through.

Above all, I realized that without God being first and foremost in my life, I am nothing. I was convicted by Jesus' words: "He who abides in me, and I in him, he it is that bears much fruit, for apart from me you can do nothing" (John 15:5).

**A Peace That Passes Understanding.** The last year and a half I've known a peace that I never had before—not when I was out of prison and not when I was in prison. It came through prayer. It came through reading the Bible and applying it to my life. Now I've really experienced what Paul wrote in the Letter to the Philippians: "By prayer and supplication with thanksgiving let your requests be made known to God. And the peace of God, which passes all understanding, will keep your hearts and your minds in Christ Jesus" (Philippians 4:6-7).

Now God is putting my relationships with my wife, my mom, my stepmother, and my stepfather back together. Even my dad, who lives in another state, knows where I am and what I'm doing.

It was when I was sick and tired of what I was doing that I finally let God change me. Until I asked Jesus into my life—and he came to me in a very big way—there was no way out. Now I want everyone else to know there is a way out for them, too. The time is now. "Right now" can be their time. ■

# 28

# "You Do Not See What I See"

### by Joseph Difato

One evening while my wife and I were reading, Christine, our three-year-old daughter, came into our room. Moments later, as she was leaving, she walked into the wall; she could not see the door. Startled, she began to cry. We realized at that moment that something was wrong with her.

We helped her back to her bed and in the morning my wife Felicia set up an appointment with an eye specialist.

After diagnostic examination, the doctor informed Felicia that Christine had bilateral retinoblastoma—cancer of the eyes—and that the tumors were quite advanced. While everything in her behavior had appeared normal until the night before, we were now confronted with the knowledge that malignant tumors were growing in both of Christine's eyes, destroying her vision.

The doctor told us that Christine had suffered significant retinal damage in her left eye. In the right eye, the retina was completely detached. The trace of good news was that only about ten percent of those diagnosed with retinoblastoma die of the disease. We were told that our daughter had about a fifty-fifty chance of retaining sight in her left eye but that tumor growth had nearly filled the right eye. There was virtually no chance that she would retain any vision in that eye.

**An Internal Battle of Faith.** The doctor wanted us to act right away, but I needed time to pray, to gather more information, and then to discern how we should proceed. In the next few days, my mind struggled against turmoil. My head was filled with thoughts about how unfair it was for a child to have to undergo such trauma; that all children should have the right to a normal, healthy life.

During the next few days, a battle raged in my mind. "What did my little girl do to deserve such a fate?" I could accept it if this had happened to an older person, to one who had been given a number of "healthy" years, but this wasn't fair. Deep down, I couldn't understand how or why God had let this happen. I knew that God has a perfect, loving plan for each person, yet I found myself asking: "How could God have such a plan for Christine? Does he really involve himself with everyone he creates, or are we at the mercy of a God who has stepped away from the world he made? Does God rule or are we subject to a blind fate which arbitrarily decides our destinies?"

As I began to pray, God showed me that he did have a plan, and that even though I did not understand it, he was in control. I recalled the story of Abraham's readiness to sacrifice Isaac at God's command. Abraham was asked to kill his only son, the gift of God through whom his descendants were to be as numerous as the stars in the sky. Surely, Abraham could not understand God's plan at that moment.

I struggled, but as I examined God's many attributes—his justice, mercy, and perfection, his unchanging nature, his omnipotence and omnipresence—I could only reaffirm that whatever God so desired or allowed to happen was for the best; in some way it would advance his plan for the salvation of all people.

At a prayer meeting the following Sunday, while the anxiety and sorrow was still very present in my heart, the Lord spoke to us in prophecy through another person:

> *My people, who knows what is best for Christine? Is it not I alone? Would I allow her, in all her innocence, to suffer unjustly for even a second? My people, I know what is best for Christine.*

After the prophecy, I experienced a true moment of grace, deep peace and joy. I was willing at that moment to say: "Your will be done, Lord." Deep inside me I knew that he had Christine in his hands and would not let her go. I could trust his plan (even though I didn't understand it), even if it meant that Christine would die. As a parent, I wanted to see Christine healed. Yet as a believer, I wanted to see God's plan fulfilled. His love moved my heart.

**A Trip to Boston.** The next day, Christine and I flew to Boston, hoping to see Fr. Ralph DiOrio, a priest with a powerful healing ministry. We drove to the priest's office and spoke to him by telephone. I explained Christine's situation, but because of an already over-extended schedule, he told us, regretfully, that he wouldn't be able to see us. He prayed for Christine over the phone. I thanked him, left Christine with some of the people there and went into the chapel to pray. A few minutes later, Fr. DiOrio called us back and told us to stay where we were. He altered his schedule to make time to come see us.

When he arrived, he celebrated a Mass for healing.

During the reading of the gospel, Fr. DiOrio felt a burning pain in his eyes and closed them tightly for about thirty seconds because of the intense pain. When he finally opened his eyes, he turned to me and said, "The Lord is going to heal this girl." After Mass, he prayed over her, anointed her with oil, gave her a toy, and we departed.

Nothing appeared to change in Christine's eyes. Who can understand the mind of God? Why does God do what he does? When does he heal? Why will he heal? While we like to see physical healing, sometimes deeper healing takes place. As I was praying on the plane ride home, I felt God telling me that while he grieved over my daughter's condition, he grieved much more over those who would suffer eternally.

**Radiation Treatments.** The next month, Christine began radiation treatment on her eyes. These treatments spanned five weeks, five days each week. When we first arrived at the children's center of Johns Hopkins University Hospital in Baltimore for tests, I was concerned for my daughter. But by the time I left that day, I could see how—because of my focus on myself and my immediate family—I had been completely out of touch with all the suffering children who are hospitalized with terminal diseases. My eyes were really opened.

My heart was filled with compassion for these children; they were so brave, and I knew God loved them deeply. I talked to, witnessed to, and prayed with some of the children. I found myself grateful to God for all that he had done in our lives, including Christine's sickness, for it had opened my eyes to a world of suffering that I had little knowledge of before.

During the radiation treatments, Felicia went to the hospital four days a week; I took Christine on the fifth. These trips usually took the entire day, most of it spent in the waiting room. We saw the same people in that room, day after day. Most were elderly; many were lonely and brokenhearted. All were undergoing radiation treatment. As we talked with them, we frequently found that they had little or no family, children, or friends to support them. Some had not seen their homes or families for months.

Since everyone had something in common, Felicia was able to use this as an opening to share the gospel. Many received her words with kindness and hope. Often they were as concerned and saddened for Christine as they were by their own difficulties. Christine was the only child undergoing radiation at that time and her situation moved them to sympathy. It also gave Felicia a wonderful opportunity to witness to them about the Lord's providence, even in trying situations. With each passing week, we grew more grateful for all the Lord had done for us.

Around this time, Christine had the opportunity to attend a healing service. She went with two other friends who were terminally ill. When the priest prayed over them, all three of them rested in the Spirit. Christine showed no sign of physical healing, but when she came home that night she told everyone, "The Spirit laid me down!"

**The Results Of the Treatments.** The radiation caused the tumors in both of Christine's eyes to shrink significantly. But, as expected, the right eye had been completed destroyed by the cancer and seven months later, it was removed. The left eye, however, seemed to be doing well. Each examination revealed that the tumor continued to shrink and the doctor was increasingly confident.

Nearly twenty months after Christine's radiation treatment, a periodic check-up exam showed that the tumor in her left eye was growing again. The next month, Christine, at four years old, lost this eye as well. At this time, Christine—an unusually outgoing child—became introverted, fearful and lethargic. Her behavior changed so dramatically that we were worried that the tumor might have spread through the optic nerve into the brain.

If this were the case, it would most likely result in her death. I was in the observation room as a CAT scan was performed to assess Christine's condition. I remember sitting in the observation room and saying to myself: "If it's over, it's over, and I'm ready. If she is going to die, if this is what you want, Lord, then this is what I want too. I want your will, Lord, not mine. If this is how Christine is going to give you glory, then so be it."

**Trusting in God.** Happily, the tests proved negative. Within two weeks, Christine stopped mourning over her condition and began to adjust. She soon learned to function with her disability. Christine is now sixteen years old. She enjoys school, loves to read in Braille, and plays the piano. We feel that Christine is every bit as happy as our other five children. We regularly pray that God will physically heal Christine. We have not lost hope.

Sometimes it still hurts me to see my daughter blind. When this happens, Felicia is quick to point out that Christine is exactly who God wants her to be. Christine is one more way that God intends to reveal his love and glory to the world. As parents, we wish and pray that Christine might see again. As Christians, we want God's will to be done, but please, Lord, do not be too demanding!

We will never be able to understand the mind of God, and yet we must trust him. Many of us know that cancer, or any illness, is filled with anxiety and suffering. It hurts! We do not have answers for why these things happen. Our only answer is to trust God.

One day, we will find out all the answers to these and many other difficult questions. On that day, when Jesus comes again in glory, we might not even care. Our minds and thoughts will be directed to the unveiling of a far greater mystery. In the meantime, don't ever challenge Christine to a race in the dark. She will beat you! ■

# Also from The Word Among Us Press:
## The New Testament
## Devotional Commentary Series

Matthew: A Devotional Commentary
Mark: A Devotional Commentary
Luke: A Devotional Commentary
John: A Devotional Commentary
Acts: A Devotional Commentary
Romans and Galatians: A Devotional Commentary
Leo Zanchettin, General Editor
Enjoy praying through the New Testament with commentaries that
include each passage of Scripture with a faith-filled meditation.

## The Wisdom Series

Love Songs: Wisdom from Saint Bernard of Clairvaux
Live Jesus! Wisdom from Saints Francis de Sales and Jane de Chantal
A Radical Love: Wisdom from Dorothy Day
My Heart Speaks: Wisdom from Pope John XXIII
Welcoming the New Millennium: Wisdom from Pope John II
Touching the Risen Christ: Wisdom from The Fathers
Walking with the Father: Wisdom from Brother Lawrence
Hold Fast to God: Wisdom from The Early Church
Even unto Death: Wisdom from Modern Martyrs

These popular books include short biographies of the authors and
selections from their writings grouped around themes such as prayer,
forgiveness, and mercy.

## To Order call 1-800-775-9673
## or order online at www.wau.org

# The Partners in Evangelism Prison Ministry

*Partners in Evangelism* is a ministry established in 1989 by The Word Among Us Inc. to meet the spiritual needs of the growing inmate population by providing solid faith-building materials to prisoners free of charge.

Because of the generosity of thousands of donors, *Partners* has continued to grow over the years. Today, more than 14,000 Catholic inmates receive *The Word Among Us Magazine* each month. Here at The Word Among Us, we often receive testimonials from prisoners who let us know just how much they appreciate this daily devotional. We are convinced that as inmates experience a personal relationship with Jesus Christ, come to know the love of their heavenly Father, and are filled with the Holy Spirit, their lives will be transformed. These changes have a rippling effect on their families—spouses, children, parents, and siblings—and reduce the rate of recidivism.

As part of our mission, *Partners in Evangelism* will be sending out copies of this book free of charge to prisoners all over the U.S. and Canada. In the future, we also plan to publish pamphlets and other materials to help prisoners live out their Christian walk.

If you are interested in becoming a *Partners in Evangelism* donor, please contact:

**In the U.S.:**
Partners in Evangelism
9639 Dr. Perry Road, #126
Ijamsville, MD 21754

**In Canada:**
Metanoia Outreach
Attn: Partners in Evangelism
Box 1107, Station F
Toronto, Ontario M4Y 2T8

Please continue to pray for the *Partners in Evangelism* ministry and for prisoners everywhere.